THE BOOK OF LIFE AFTER DEATH:
ESSAYS & POEMS

Edited by Tim Lindner

Tolsun Books
Flagstaff, Las Vegas, Philadelphia

The Book of Life After Death: Essays & Poems
Copyright © 2023 by Tolsun Books. All rights reserved.
Printed in the United States of America. First Edition.

For more information, contact Tolsun Books at info@tolsunbooks.com.

Edited by Tim Lindner.
Cover art by Heather-Lang Cassera.
Cover design by David Pischke.

Set in Cochin and Democratica OT.
Design by David Pischke.

No part of this book may be used or reproduced in any manner whatsoever without the prior written permission of the copyright holder except for brief quotations in critical articles or reviews.

ISBN 978-1-948800-65-5

Published by Tolsun Publishing, Inc.,
Flagstaff, Arizona; Las Vegas, Nevada; Philadelphia, Pennsylvania.
www.tolsunbooks.com

Me and you, we got more yesterday than anybody.
We need some kind of tomorrow.

Toni Morrison

CONTENTS

vii   *Editor's Note*, Tim Lindner

2   *This Is Where*, Elizabeth Quiñones-Zaldaña

4   *Dive In*, Pam Anderson

14   *Ghazal: The Footbridge Over the Somes*, Steve Wilson

15   *Bone Man*, Nancy Gott

17   *Words Not Spoken*, Ellen Sollinger Walker

20   *Stay*, Arnisha Royston

21   *Día de los Muertos*, Robert René Galván

23   *Memento Mori, Vanitas, Tempus Fugit; Or: Shane Can't Die of Liver Cancer Because That Asshole Is Supposed To Clean Through This Asshole's Shit When I Die*, Flower Conroy

24   *Her Puzzle Page*, Farnaz Fatemi

26   *Feeding Coosah His Sugar*, Deidra Suwanee Dees

28   *All Sales Are Final*, Andrew Revie

29   *Santa Rosa*, Bryan Price

30   *Yesterday*, Ms.AyeVee

32   *My Mother, the Witch*, Courtney Harler

33   *Ten-Item Questionnaire for My Great-Grandmother*, Dani Putney

34   *A Final Resting Place*, Susan Cohen

40   *Day After Day of The Dead*, Alexis Ivy

41   *Hungry Ghosts Festival*, Kelly Kaur

42   *Major Magic's Animatronic Band*, Andrew Collard

44   *House of Cards*, Paul Skenazy

51   *Greenhouse Ghosts*, Chloe Biggs

52   *With Arthur After the Memorial for His Wife*, Xiaoly Li

54   *Retirement*, C. Prudence Arceneaux

55   *Consideration of Burial*, Flynn Dexter

56 *The Flinch Factor*, Rebecca Douglas
58 *Disco Balls & Frank Sinatra*, Audrey Forbes
59 *Elegy for a Gambler*, Jen Karetnick
61 *Reasons Why Ghosts Exist*, Arthur Kayzakian
63 *I'm Tired of Killing You*, Hunter Hazelton
65 *A Craft Talk*, Colin Pope
72 *Letter To Christa McAuliffe, in Space*, Sarah Johnson
74 *Welcoming the Light*, Jesse Arthur Stone
75 *Mujeres Divinas/Divine Women*, Sarah Chavera Edwards
77 *Channeling Mother*, Charlene Stegman Moskal
78 *Thaw*, Leah Claire Kaminski
80 *Roses In His Cheeks*, Lisa del Rosso
83 *Dead Letter*, Cathleen Calbert
84 *The Loft*, Will Stenberg
85 *Calaverita a Mi Vieja Versión*, Dulce Solis
87 *Here & Now*, Letisia Cruz
90 *Even Heaven Requires Your Survival*, Susan L. Leary
91 *Mariner*, Emilee Wirshing
92 *Deluge*, James Joseph Brown
93 *Questions on Death*, Shane Mason
94 *Once Upon a Dream Dress*, Kelly Jean Fitzsimmons
101 *Reprieve*, Linda Michel Cassidy
102 *Buffer*, DeAnna Beachley
104 *The Cradle*, Celia Lisset Alvarez
106 *Ropa Vieja y ROM the Spaceknight: En La Casa de Abuela*, Jarret Keene
116 *To My Granny*, Maeve Holler
117 *The Train Tracks Reached*, Stacey Balkun

EDITOR'S NOTE
Tim Lindner

My father grew up in a house built in 1740 in Scotch Plains, New Jersey, his parents being big history buffs. The house was full of historic artifacts, like cannonballs from the revolutionary war, old cooking equipment, classic pewter. They believed the house was haunted and one of my grandfather's life missions was to show the world that Benedict Arnold was not a traitor, but a true American patriot.

When my grandfather passed away and my grandmother lived there alone, she labeled everything in the house with index cards, both the historical items and my grandfather's writings and possessions. She famously gave any visitor a tour of the rooms: the uneven floors, the fireplaces, the heavy trinkets, and paintings hanging from the walls. One wall was covered in this brick wallpaper to make it feel even more authentic.

When she passed away, the wallpaper came down, and we had to parse the value of the items, both sentimental and monetary. My immediate family and I, the only remaining descendants, couldn't figure out what was real and what wasn't. There were letters between generals in wars, unpublished manuscripts along with rejection letters from publishers, a fake doctorate degree, replicas of historical items mixed with the authentic. To them, it was all real. To us, we had to redefine *essential* as we learned more about who my grandparents were.

The thing is, we're all going to die. So many of us spend our living years trying to control our images while we're here as we estimate and design how we'll be remembered. And we're surrounded by the dead all the time, so we should know that, despite our efforts, it's those who are still here on earth, along with our objects and artifacts, that get to shape who we are once we're gone. To craft our ghosts, if you will.

We spend all this time on earth creating our identities, revising our histories, to be remembered in a way that matches how we view ourselves. My grandfather, who suffered greatly from anxiety and depression, left no trace of those struggles. And my grandmother, the creator, and caretaker of his ghost, preserved everything exactly as he

The Book of Life After Death

wanted himself and their home to be remembered.

When we die, we have no control over who we are anymore. It's the living that decide the traits and actions that we'll think about on the birthdays of the dead, the holidays. But I think, when we hear a creaking floorboard or a tap on the window, it's those other qualities, the reality of who we once were, that haunt the living, because I imagine life after death comes with just as much nuance as our years alive; and that's OK.

I think about death a lot. I have to imagine we all do, despite what my therapist might say. This collection contains stories and poems about life after death, told by the living as we learn our responsibility for those left behind. It opens with lines by Elizabeth Quiñones-Zaldaña:

> *This is where fresh water*
> *replaces cigarettes, insulin*
> *injections, everything*
> *subject to the dry spell.*

And that's exactly it. Everything is subject to this new design, creating a multiverse of ghosts as we want to remember them, how we think the dead might want to be remembered. Throughout the collection, you'll find unfinished crossword puzzles, cobwebs, train tracks, clothing, windows, losses, and gravestones, all told through unique perspectives, hoping to define the dead in some way, whether this reveals just a shoulder fragment or the whole white sheet. Each representation is a reflection of the emotions that we can only try to express. Later in the collection, Letisia Cruz writes:

> This is how we are made to remember. Loss marks us in ways we are never prepared for. Love is the ocean spilling on the shore. Again and again. Here and now and never after. Storms pass through us. We endure our own apocalypses. And if we are lucky, we were home once.

We do endure, somehow, and maybe home is and always will be just a memory.

viii

Essays & Poems

The house in Scotch Plains has since been replaced by a new house with a bright yard with a swing set. My family and I still have the three cannonballs: one for my sister and her family, one for my parents, and one for me. We don't really know if they're authentic; we just know the story of how they found them by the fruit stand that's now an Exxon, half buried. But that's not important. Sometimes, with our ghosts, the story is all that matters.

THE BOOK OF LIFE AFTER DEATH:
ESSAYS & POEMS

THIS IS WHERE

Elizabeth Quiñones-Zaldaña

This is where fresh water
replaces cigarettes, insulin
injections, everything
subject to the dry spell.

Sunlight on the breeze
recovers the needles,
turns them to evergreen
visible, though barely,
where the sand changes color.

I am terrified
to enter the water.
There are no footprints
in the riverbed.

Songs from memory, songs
from before I was born
vie with every careless move
of my body.

When I was a child
I couldn't bear to bring my face
beneath the surface.
One summer a saltwater wave swept over me
I pushed off from the bottom,
a first breath. The experiment
could be repeated;

but there is nothing gradual
in the currents that encircle me.
There is no pattern
for me to observe.

Essays & Poems

Strangers and family
who came this way
are an abstraction,
and over the rush at my ears
what do ministering angels say?
The voice of contending prophets
entangles with theirs. My heart stops.

Those who have not seen
rest easy in their beds.
They fall asleep in a posture of peace,

but I can neither deny who I am,
nor what I've seen. So help me.
So help me —
as my face is submerged,
take me to your city.

DIVE IN
Pam Anderson

In the photo, I am mid-air, arms flung above my head, legs splayed with forward movement. I am wearing a brightly flowered red, yellow, and orange swimsuit, and although my thighs look chubby and my middle is thick, the photo's essence overrides this.

We—my husband and I—had been on a sticky tour guide-led hike in Punta Cana, all ferns and fauna. The photo marks the final stop: a cave with a deep pool of cool, clear water, a welcome relief from the unrelenting sun and heat. A well-worn platform at least ninety feet high—as tall as any high dive I had ever tiptoed out on as a pre-teen at our local pool—stretched over the water. My husband, not a swimmer, deferred to the steps as did others, but I opted for the platform.

With the rest who had made the bolder choice, I waited anxiously in the line. I shifted my weight back and forth, peeking around the snaking line to watch each person decide on a form and then proceed, either jack-knifing or cannon-balling; a few rule-breakers took several running steps and went in headfirst—disregarding the NO DIVING signs—to echoed claps and whistles.

When it was my turn and my toes finally curled around the edge of the wooden planks, I paused involuntarily: *where did this uncharacteristic bravery come from?*

I leapt.

For eight seconds of free fall nirvana, I felt many things: unencumbered, capable, strong. My toes, knees, hips, shoulders, then head submerged deep into the blue-gray water, beams of light and swirl all around me. I felt a momentary pause of reality—time stopped as the water pressed and rearranged my physical mass—before I kicked and reached upward. Then I popped above the surface, drew in a breath, pulled myself out of the pool.

I returned to the platform again and again, until it was time to leave.

A week later, I sat visiting my son in Florida. We were having a box-of-white-wine conversation, the kind that starts on the surface, but swirls deeper and deeper into pressure-filled spaces. I talked of my recent vacation a bit, then pulled up the photo of me leaping from the platform to show him.

"You look like your mom," he laughed. "Did you borrow that swimsuit from Grandma?" Deflated that what Matt saw was merely his mother plopping into a pool in a matronly swimsuit, I tried to explain to him how *free* I had felt in that moment. My son leaned in, assuring me he was teasing, then listened as I tried to capture the essence of the moment—a freedom I hadn't felt in a long while—into words. Realizing this was important to me, he nodded along and said, "That's great, Mom."

On many Saturdays while I was in elementary or junior high school, I would sit on the front steps, shaded by the mature elm trees, reading a library book as my father cut our small postage stamp-sized lawn with the push mower. He would wear his "chores" outfit, a dad-standard for the mid-70's: denim shorts that hit mid-thigh with dark dress socks, dark work shoes, and a white tank t-shirt.

After the lawn, he would tend to the impatiens and the petunias he had planted on the side of the limestone house along the narrow driveway. It was the only space that had any decent sun exposure, but often the edges of the flowers would get run over if someone drove up to the garage behind the house too quickly or carelessly.

My mom worked from home as a medical transcriptionist during the week, but on the weekend she would take her typed reports to file at the hospital, so Dad spent Saturdays at home with us kids. On most Saturdays at home, we headed inside only after the afternoon sun began to wane; Dad's policy was no indoor chores if it was nice outside, a habit I still maintain to this day.

In the privacy of the indoors, my father would put on a hairnet to tame his cowlicks for church in the morning, pressing down the belligerent edges of the grown-out crewcut that he'd wore during the 50's and 60's. The black puckered stem of the hairnet sat in the middle of his forehead like a bindi, making the general appearance that much sillier on my Methodist father, but it was something we were all used to. My mother was a beauty routine minimalist, but my father doted on his appearance with his menagerie of concoctions, hair oils and after shaves, skin lotions and scented soaps.

The Book of Life After Death

Later in the day, I might sit at the table in the kitchen as my dad prepared a meatloaf or casserole; after dinner, he would get on his hands and knees to scrub the gold checkered linoleum floor. Organ music would pour from the stereo system—never loudly though; we lived too close to neighbors and my parents were considerate people. Then, kitchen chores complete, my father would head down to the basement laundry room to iron the next week's dress shirts into crisp white perfection.

In those days, I understood my dad's routines, his eccentricities, his moods. When I was young, it seemed then as if there was not anything I did not know about my father.

Another glass of wine deeper into conversation, my son looked at me as if I were crazy.

"That *was* his job in the army. He was a cook," I repeated.

"Mom, no. Grandpa was mortar squad. He was in an advance company, one of the first regiments into Korea. That means Grandpa would've been about fifty feet back from the front line, prepping for mortar launches."

My son had been close with my dad and had a keen interest in military history. As a boy, he had been fascinated by my dad's olive army uniform that hung surrounded by mothballs in the upstairs closet, and often wore the jacket when he played at my parents' home. But though he knew a lot about my dad, I was certain he was confused about this. I called my mom to verify.

"Your *dad* wasn't a cook in the army," she confirmed. "My *brother* was a cook for the marines. Maybe that's why you are mixed up? Mortar squad sounds right. I didn't know your dad yet when he served in Korea, but I do know he had nightmares for many years. He didn't much want to talk about that time, though. It's a part of his life he kept private."

I hung up with my mother and my chest felt tight, my breath knocked out of me. I felt adrift, unmoored, both because I couldn't imagine my dad performing any violent act, and also because there were chunks of his life about which I knew nothing.

"How did *you* know these things about my dad?"

"I researched his service records a few years after he died," my son said, "but Grandpa used to tell me stories. I remember he talked about the whistles—why he hated *whistles*. The Koreans would blow them throughout the night, playing mind games. Grandpa's unit was always on alert in case the whistles were a signal for an oncoming attack. Grandpa said no one got a good night's sleep, ever."

Contemplating how lonely it must have been for my dad to have kept so much of this to himself, I reached over and touched my son's wrist, a rush of wine-soaked love coursing through me, thankful for the intimacy they had shared, thankful that *someone* knew this part of my dad's story.

My father suffered a heart attack—and lost his job because of extended recovery time—when I was in high school, and he was in his late fifties. He was too young to retire, but too old to easily find a new mid-level management position. I understand now that it was personally humbling and financially devastating—although my parents never talked about such things with us kids—and that this drawn-out job-seeking period exposed and then enhanced significant fault lines in my parents' marriage: neither was living the life they envisioned for themselves.

Eventually, my dad reinvented himself after he took a job with a neighbor who owned a limousine and hearse leasing company. Once he started this job my dad dove into it entirely, driving private cars for trips to the airport, limos for celebrations, and hearses for funerals. He never turned down any livery job, but of all options, my dad preferred funerals. He was a man of manners, always helping a person off with her coat, pulling out a chair for someone, holding out an arm to guide a person to the door. Those life skills apply in the funeral world, where people are disoriented and wobbly with grief.

As my dad got older, he only drove hearses. He got tired of the drunken celebration of weddings and proms, and in truth, he was a serious man, much more suited to the quiet calm of the funeral world. He would lead the grieving from the car, gracefully handling their coats as well as their dignity. The funeral directors appreciated my dad because he always wanted to help; he was never one to wait outside like many of the other drivers, leaning against the hearse smoking a cigarette.

The Book of Life After Death

After a decade of being constantly "on call", when he was in his later sixties, my dad left the leasing company to work for one specific funeral home. He enjoyed the company of the owners and employees and he often stayed back to chat—sometimes for hours—once a funeral had ended. My dad was not a man who had friends, not really. While my peers' dads would have buddies over to watch sports on a portable TV in the garage, drinking beer and using language they couldn't use inside their homes, my dad was less raw, more formal; his main social events were Wednesday night church choir practice and Sunday morning services.

At the funeral home, my dad befriended one employee in particular, John, who was significantly younger—in his mid-thirties. When, it seemed, the hours of conversation at the funeral home weren't enough, my dad would talk with John for hours on our centrally located house phone—decades before the cell phone offered access to secrecy—often late into the night. My family, my mom, my two brothers and I, seemed to have a tacit agreement that we would separately and privately ignore these calls during which my father spoke to John in startlingly low, urgent tones, and even occasionally giggled; I am certain I had never heard my dad giggle before.

When I was in my mid-twenties and about to be married, my dad hired a limousine from the company that he had worked for; he requested that John be the driver. On my wedding day, John arrived early, so my dad invited him in as we made final preparations before leaving the house. It felt unnatural that John was in our living room while professional pre-wedding photos were being shot of me, my family, my bridesmaids, but I ignored that feeling; I had more important things on my mind that day. At the time it registered only a little when, later in the night, I noted my non-drinking dad with a glass of whiskey, his bow tie undone and the top buttons of his dress shirt open, and then later still, when my dad and John were fast dancing near the DJ. My dad's hands were in fists, making small circular motions as he swayed his body, beads of sweat across his forehead, his eyes half-closed.

Remembering that day now, it's strange to think that packed away somewhere in my garage is the wedding album from my first marriage that includes photos of John, a ghost to me now, first captured standing in our living room, then beaming at the camera with my dad standing next to him as he ceremoniously opened the door of the limo for the bride, then in a photo from the reception, my parents seated at dinner in the foreground, with John at another table in the background, looking over in my dad's direction.

My son and I moved out onto the balcony of the Florida hotel room I was staying in, drinking our wine in small, plastic cups. The ocean broke, then swashed in front of us; the night breeze chilled our bare feet that we had propped up on the wrought-iron slats fencing the balcony. We had already dived into many topics beyond my vacation and my dad's military service—our current work and our relationships, goals we had set, the state of our happiness—but something in his voice as he opened a new lane of conversation created the unnerving sensation of bubbles floating furiously, then colliding behind my sternum.

"Mom. There is something I've been meaning to ask you," he began, then paused.

I waited.

"I know the story I was told when I was twelve—your divorce with dad was a *mutual decision*—and you've both maintained that, but I'd like to know something. Who *initiated* the divorce? One of you had to want it *first*."

Back when my first husband and I split up, divorced friends had shared sage advice: *your children only get one mom, they only get one dad.* Despite our disparate views of what went wrong and why, we had agreed that we would never pit our children against the other parent, we would never disrespect one another to them. With few and minor exceptions, we have held to that. Once, a few years back, I rambled out a frustration about his dad, and Matt shut me down, saying, "Mom, yes, Dad can be an asshole. But he's also *more than* just an asshole." Since then, I try not to make that mistake.

For the well-being of their children, parents keep parts of their lives private. With my own children, I tiptoed around the topic of my divorce, because I didn't know what my now-adult children may know—what they may have learned beyond the narrative we had offered them—about the year leading up to our separation and divorce.

The Book of Life After Death

At a broad glance, it is true that our marriage's end *was* a mutual decision, the result of our not leading the life either of us had envisioned.

But it was also true that, in that final year, I had been pulled into the chaotic riptide of an affair. That I had felt seen and heard and desired for the first time in many years, and because of this, I desperately wanted my marriage to be over. That I had also been betrayed repeatedly—my lover was also married and had no immediate plan to leave his wife. That I had built barriers with the bricks of heavy lies between myself and everyone close to me. That I had kept many of these lies in place so as not to cause unnecessary harm to anyone.

Within the ocean of all these details, to answer the question honestly: it was *me* who wanted out first, because I was in love with another man. Did I want my son to know this about me?

I walked out onto the platform and curled my toes around the edge.

"It is true that your dad and I made a mutual decision…" My son rolled his eyes, but I touched his arm, indicating I had more to say. "But, before our marriage was over, I was already in love with Parker."

My dad's friendship with John seemed to hit a crescendo around the time of my wedding, then dissipated as my dad got older and started to get phased out of hearse work. One afternoon Dad significantly damaged a hearse backing into a cement wall, and that was the beginning of the end of his second career.

Perhaps to replace the loss of John, in the senior condo community where my parents had by then moved, my dad forged new relationships with other men: one friendship with "the boys", a couple who together owned a nearby video store, and another friendship with an elderly bachelor who my dad frequently dropped in on. He fawned over these friends, laughing loudly, leaning in intently, not just to listen to their stories it seemed, but almost to let the details soak into him, to be saturated by them.

My mom would sometimes scold my dad ("Give the boys some space!") or occasionally share with me how embarrassed she was by his behavior. I imagine, though, that it hurt to see that Dad always seemed liveliest when he was with others, away from their life together—even then, after almost fifty years of marriage—although she rarely betrayed my dad with any unkind words to him or about him. My

Essays & Poems

parents were, from beginning to end, unfailingly polite to one another.

"Well, that changes everything," Matt said. "I always thought it was Dad who wanted out." I had been holding my breath, expecting a judgement that might match the shame I had borne for years.

His comment surprised me; I exhaled fully, furrowed my brow.

"What made you think that?"

"Because he started dating his college girlfriend—the one before you—right after you guys split. I just assumed they had been having an affair."

It was true that my first husband had started dating within weeks of our separation. At the time, though, my ex had told me that he met Mary, his instant girlfriend, on a ski-trip to Montana he had taken to "clear his head" the week after he moved out. With this new knowledge—that his relationship didn't begin as a chance meeting with a stranger but was probably a pre-arranged visit with an old flame—my head began to spin.

I felt as if I were in a low-budget film's rewind montage. Mary lived in Montana, and she travelled back and forth for a few months before she eventually moved in with my ex about six months later—and with my children for half of the time.

I sat with this new information, angry, trying to piece together why I had never thought twice about the flimsiness of the "meeting on the ski hill" tale. Overwhelmed, I was drowning in secrets.

My question for my son, "Wait...you said *This changes everything*. What did you mean?"

"I've been wondering for a while...maybe he and Mary had been having an affair... you know, maybe you weren't first choice...maybe he didn't want the life he had, but felt he couldn't leave..."

Hearing Matt's fragility, even at age twenty-seven, wondering whether his dad saw his family, his children, as an impediment to the life he had wanted, my lungs constricted into tight fists, making it hard to breathe. Every detail I had been trying to sort out vanished; I focused on the only part of the story that mattered.

"No, Matt. I have no idea if Dad and Mary had been in touch—maybe they had—but it wouldn't have been until the very end of our time together—and it had nothing to do with *you*, with *wanting* you

11

kids, with *loving* you kids. *I'm* the one who checked out…It was *me*."

Matt looked over at me, considering this. There was much for both Matt and I to sift through, a lot we hadn't known and needed to sit with, but tonight wasn't the time.

Feeling rearranged, I studied the ocean, comprised of beams of light and swirl.

Then I stood, reached upward with a stretch, and took a deep breath. "Come on, let's go inside. It's getting cold."

In his eighties, my dad's body and memory began to fail him, and my mother cared diligently for him for several years while he was in and out of hospitals. Although it had been clear late in their marriage that my mother had years of resentment bottled up, an unspoken settling transpired between them during this time: equilibrium seemed restored once my dad relied on my mom for almost everything. He needed her, and she needed him to need her.

After my dad passed, I helped my mom clear out my dad's things, deciding what was to be donated, given to family members, or tossed away. We found boxes in the attic in which my dad had saved photos and memorabilia from his youth, from his time in the service, from his many years as a husband, and father, and grandfather. I saved a few items of his sentimental collection, including letters commending his service in Korea, now stored in my own boxes of memories.

My mother and I also unearthed a secret stash Dad had squirreled away in a cedar chest: expensive dress shirts, crisp white handkerchiefs, shiny cubic zirconia rings, and a large collection—a virtual video library—of gay pornography. The neat rows of VHS and DVD covers stabbed at my gut like a dull knife. We sat silently until my mother, ever private with her heart, simply asked that they be disposed of. Immediately.

In the years since his death, I've had to make peace with an alternate version of my father, the version that he was most likely a closeted gay man. It would take time for me to digest, despite the reality that on some level, I already *knew* about the layers of clues scattered throughout our lives. I just hadn't been able to acknowledge them.

It was hard to consider that my dad was unable to fully be the person who he really was. It made me sad, and it made me angry, both

Essays & Poems

with him and for him. It made me wonder if I—if any of us—had really known him at all, if *he* had resented the life he had.

One thing I do know: my dad, like me, loved sunshine and he loved water. Once he had officially retired, for two months of every year, my dad would travel to different locations in Florida. He hated the cold and my mother was still working full-time—at the time these solitary vacations seemed to make sense. Because I often joined him for a week during these trips, I know that my father would sit by the pool and read, then later take long walks down the beach, working on his tan, occasionally shielding his eyes and gazing out into the distance. He never ventured far into the water, though, as my dad had never learned to swim.

Still, my father, like me, seemed drawn to waves' secrets—some of which, worn smooth from being tossed relentlessly about, eventually washed up onto the sand, and some of which remained buried deep on the ocean's floor.

The Book of Life After Death

GHAZAL:
THE FOOTBRIDGE OVER THE SOMES
Steve Wilson

Autumn arrives, with night perching on my open window.
I watch workers shuffle home, a foreigner at an open window.

When winter retreats, the melting ice reflects like glass—
I wander out. A woman's robe hangs at a half-open window.

The river, alive beneath the bridge, swims over rocks, bottles,
an empty barrel. What words you whispered at your open window.

Years ago, armies took these streets. "Which side were you on?"
I ask Ferenc, my old neighbor. His face is an open window.

Beside one bank or the other, children play in the alleyways.
I'm alone, waving to ghosts through this open window.

—Cluj, Romania

Essays & Poems

BONE MAN

Nancy Gott

I. You
hold a bag in your hands,
take out bones one by one.
Seek the marrow of memory.
Construct a poem from this rubble.

II. Me
My body wants to go where you are,
wants to breathe you in.
Oh, essential element of ash,
whose unrequited sigh is this?

III. We
argued over there,
where the virus found
in Foucault's body found you,
turned you into bone.

IV. Bone
I kick you with my shoe,
uproot you from your grave,
fly you across this ocean.
You sing at 3 a.m.

V. Ghost
From your throat
words spring forth
weightless as water
washing bones.

VI. You
are here,

15

The Book of Life After Death

present in this poem
left behind,
and found.

Essays & Poems

WORDS NOT SPOKEN
Ellen Sollinger Walker

1.

The first time a picture fell off a wall in our house, I had just gotten out of the shower. Chris, my husband, was just waking up when I yelled, "What was that?" Chris had already been diagnosed with a terminal lung disease by this time, and suffered from a cough I had once called his "pot cough," until I knew better. He slowly rolled over and turned on the light. A painting had broken its string and crashed down onto the glass dog bowl below it, smashing it and spewing water everywhere.

"Wow, the spirits must be angry about something this morning," I quipped, combing my wet hair.

Driving to work, "Whiskey in the Jar" came on the radio and I turned it up and sang along:

> *In walked Captain Farrell*
> *I jumped up, fired my pistols*
> *And I shot him with both barrels.*
>
> *Whack for my daddy, oh!*
> *Whack for my daddy, oh!*
> *There's whiskey in the jar, oh*

The minute I got to work, my cell phone rang. It was Chris. His voice sounded wobbly and serious.

"David died in a car accident last night."

"Oh, no," I whispered and then my heart dipped like a kite that has lost its air, hitting the ground, all spineless and flimsy.

David, Chris' fifteen-year-old nephew, was always happy, with a wide, goofy grin on his face.

When he was three years old, David's father shot his mother's lover

17

The Book of Life After Death

and then shot himself in the head. "There was one more bullet in the chamber," David's mother would remind us after drinking too much beer and downing too many Jell-O shots. "That last bullet was meant for me."

2.

Chris and I were married on 11/11/11. There was a full moon that night. Elevens and perfectly round, full moons were always good omens for us. With Chris, I felt reborn and alive. I loved the warmth of his skin under my fingers. I loved his talent for charming people into doing things for him. I loved how, once, when two bald eagles were circling above our house, Chris lay with me in the grass to watch them perform their graceful waltz above us on a bright blue dance floor.

Chris was hospitalized in December 2013. The lung disease was clogging the delicate membranes, causing him to slowly suffocate. He looked sweet in his green hospital gown while Stella, our poodle, snuggled down in his sheets. A few days before he died, the nurse put him in a recliner like he was royalty, accepting guests. Friends came to visit, old railroad buddies and their kids. I could see the sparkle in Chris' gray-blue eyes slowly fading, like a chameleon who loses his color on drab, gray stone.

That night, I tried to tell him he was going to die soon, because no one, including his doctors and nurses, had ever said those words to him.

But, I couldn't say them either. "You will be with God soon," was all I could get out. What a stupid thing to say. Then, the ventilator was thrust down his throat and that was the last time I ever heard his voice.

3.

Chris died at Christmastime so we couldn't give each other presents. The present he never got was a photograph I took on our trip to Glacier National Park, reprinted on canvas. After his death, I unwrapped it and hung it on our wall by the fireplace. When I got home from work one

Essays & Poems

night, the picture had fallen off the wall and lay, right-side up, on the floor. Without much thought, I rehung the picture in the same place, making sure it was firmly planted on the hook. The next night after work, the Glacier picture was, again, on the floor. I felt a momentary heart-bomb-burst but, undeterred, I hung it on a different hook. On the third night after work, the Glacier picture remained stationary but a larger photograph, a wedding present in glass, was lying on the floor, face up, directly below its hook. It seemed as if someone had carefully lifted the picture off the wall and, with great love, placed it on the floor.

A few weeks later, I was talking on the phone to a friend about the just-discovered financial disaster Chris left for me after his death. A $45,000 debt that he accrued without my knowledge was now my responsibility to pay back. I was telling my friend how angry I was and "Why would he leave me in this horrible situation?" That night while I was watching television, a painting Chris and I had bought together, which was hanging in the bedroom, crashed to the floor with an aggressive, out-of-control smash.

"Christ!" I yelled out loud and an unbridled fear shot up my spine.

4.

A friend gave me some wrapped, dried sage and instructed me how to perform the Native American "smudging" ceremony. I discovered, after some research, that the purpose of "smudging" was to wash away dark thoughts and unwanted energy or emotion that may cling to a space after someone's death. That evening, I lit the dried sage like a cigar and walked around my house, allowing the smoke, which smelled like ancient cedar, to float into all the corners of all the rooms. I said gentle words to Chris like "Please find peace and leave this house." Tibetan finger chimes were also part of my smudging ceremony, an ethereal, heavenly sound rose up to the ceiling with the smoke.

The next day, I was entertaining a friend and I reached into the bottom of a cabinet where I kept my favorite dishes. There, hidden away behind the plates, was my unwrapped Christmas present from Chris, a beautiful silver necklace with a cross, made of bright white opals, hanging gently from its chain. Each opal was oval-shaped and luminous, like an imperfect, warped, full moon.

STAY

Arnisha Royston

If   we had   more   time
i would   have stayed   held
your hand   when   you felt   like
dying   and even   after   you died
or became   something   darker
like   magic   or   wet   fist
and   cold baths   or   old
broken   radios   and   wired
wrist   i would   have   stayed
watched you   rot   then   measure
the distance   between   our bed
as you   tried to   pull   yourself
back   together   dragging   the
corners   of   your hands   across

if   there is   more   time
stay   hold your   hands   above
your head   alive or   dead
become   something darker   like
magic   or   space   teach yourself
to   disappear   to make   music

with your   fist   in lonely   closets
next to   rusty nails   listen   to
the clawing   watch   as the   skin
under   your nails   begins   to
peel   wire it   shut
let   the distance   between
 us   grow   i will   escape
this time   you stay   for   yourself.

Essays & Poems

DÍA DE LOS MUERTOS

Robert René Galván

Mariposas
have returned
for thousands
of years,
painting the sky
like a stained-glass
window,
long before the shining
men arrived with steel
and banners,
desires
and superstitions.

Marigolds rise
in the fields
like orange suns,
the fragrance
draws the dead
from *Mictlán*,
fill *ofrendas*
with light
among gifts
of *chocolate*
and
Pan de Muerto,
pulque and *mezcal*,
hibiscus water
and a pinch
of salt
for the weary
traveler.

The Book of Life After Death

The streets host
calaveras
and *papel picado*,
vendors of *tamales*
and *champarrado* –
a joyous festival
to greet migrant souls,
unlike émigré rites
in the cathedral
of purloined stones
and syncretic clouds
of *copal*.

By morning
the incense clears
and *esquincles* guide
our ancestors back
to *Chimalma's*
open arms
in a dark and distant
realm.

Essays & Poems

MEMENTO MORI, VANITAS, TEMPUS FUGIT; OR:
SHANE CAN'T DIE OF LIVER CANCER BECAUSE THAT ASSHOLE IS SUPPOSED TO CLEAN THROUGH THIS ASSHOLE'S SHIT WHEN I DIE
Flower Conroy

Don't worry I burned most of those journals we mailed to Florida from Jersey—the return postage claiming to be from Pasty Cline in case anyone read those tortured pages—because of course of her song. But there are other journals you'll have to pour over. Marginalia scribbled in books. I don't know what to tell you about my vintage wardrobe of—how did you put it, ugly clothes that I love? The boxes of photos. You know what photos I mean. Bust out the gasoline. Computer files—you'll go bananas trying to suss that out—trash from garbage, revision of revision of revision of. On second thought maybe you can drum up a scandal with some of those photos. But don't use any that aren't me alone. I'm not dragging anyone down with me—just myself. This would be easier if I didn't have to think about your bile bag. Or you taking a Scotch-Brite Lint Roller to your balding head. That *was* funny. Two words: Browser History. I know you've walked me through deleting that but. You know: technology. Also—I thought the artifacts of my afterlife would be a bit more compelling but it turns out I'm mostly vapid, self-absorbed, and not very discerning. I mean I didn't even bother to collect the good bad thrift store art. And all those craft projects—the vases I was going to affix into abstract garden totems? The bins of plastic dinosaurs I was going to what—what was I going to do with them? I feel like a ghost. Hard to remember. My knuckles won't crack. Eyesight worsening. The deal was you were going to do this for me. I would be able to die and you'd pick up the pieces. That was the deal.

The Book of Life After Death

HER PUZZLE PAGE

Farnaz Fatemi

1 Across, Clue, *Go*.
She's filled in the six-letter DEPART.

Top row, right side: three-letter ZAG.
Clue, *Make a sharp turn*.

For four years, pushed into
my bedside drawer: her last

handwriting a mix of lower and upper case,
black ink, her thinking in the scrawl.

What got finished: *the place Madonna
was recently denied an adoption*. How did she know this?

And how couldn't she see that *one who investigates*,
P_O_ _ R, is a prober, of course.

Verklempt person's cry:
she knew it: OY VEY.

The thing I know, she's left blank:
the recently dead pitcher's team.

She might have laughed at this
or marveled I could translate *Ardor*

into the four-letter ZEAL.
I imagine her mouthing

clues aloud: *"Capeesh?"* and
—a fitting response—I SEE.

24

Essays & Poems

Her alphabets entice:
If I ink the letters in now,

the page would silence,
puzzle completed.

The answers she didn't finish,
but would have

with time: Clue, *Heretofore*.
She wrote: ERE_OW.

FEEDING COOSAH HIS SUGAR

Deidra Suwanee Dees

"Otis, *Otis!* Come here, *Otis!*" she called. Otis climbed down from the skinny dogwood that barely supported his lanky frame. Running up the back steps, jacket flapping, he burst through the big door; screen door slamming behind him.

Into the warm kitchen, holding out his cupped hand, Otis's mother, Mama Bell, piled on the lumpy brown sugar almost brimming over. "You take this sugar to Coosah, *Otis, okay?*" Looking straight into his dark Muscogee eyes, Mama Bell said, "You feed *all this sugar to the horse — you hear me?*"

"Yes ma'am," Otis said, closing the kitchen door with one hand, steadying the other not to let the screen door hit it. As he walked to the barn in the fall afternoon, through the cool air his nose caught a scent of the molasses sugar balancing in his right hand.

Otis thought, "How good that sugar would taste! Like candy the white kids brought to school in their lunch pails. Like lollipops in The Big Store that Indians couldn't afford."

As he walked into the barn — shadowed, dark, out of eye-shot of Mama Bell — he pushed his face headlong into the pile of sugar taking the biggest bite he could get. Rocky, gritty, then melting like syrup, sliding down his throat — sugar rush.

Otis shoved his right hand under the horse's mouth saying, "Coosah, here's your sugar, ole boy. Pretty boy, gentle boy." With the other hand, he rubbed Coosah's face — nibbling, slobbering, vapor rising.

Coosah looked up seeming to ask, "Where's the rest of my sugar?" He nudged the side of Otis's head, wetting his stringy long hair — sugar ear. Otis halfway ducked — catching himself, thinking he really shouldn't be bothered by Coosah's slobber. After all, he thought, "It was a small price to pay for stealing the horse's sugar."

So was the story of feeding Coosah his sugar. My father, who was the young boy named Otis, told me this story many times when I was growing up. Every time he told the story, his dark Muscogee eyes, set deep in his head, became fixed upon the past. His face grew coarse

Essays & Poems

seeming to stumble upon discomfort at the story's end. "I believe that was the only time — *the only time* — I ever disobeyed my mother," he said.

Choking silence followed. Awkwardness. I always felt sorry for daddy not really knowing what to say. He never spoke of it, but I knew Mama Bell had died shortly after she sent him out to feed Coosah his sugar.

Now, when I tell the story to my children, I come to that same silence at the story's end. Awkwardness returns. Daddy died shortly after telling me the story... neither of us realizing it was the very last time he would tell the story about feeding Coosah his sugar.

ALL SALES ARE FINAL

Andrew Revie

Effigies left on the sallow map of the body.

The beginning as short as the end was long.

The muse's song a sepulcher to his wayward mouth.

Plundered from such minimum catastrophes.

She became an ark brimming with thresholds.

Beheld in the crowning of dawns.

With thousand-yard stares hung from the nightstand.

Who can say we are not our own means and ends?

Where the faithful sundered and myth was in turn.

In text messages poised like daggers.

From shuttered windows we are all beholden to.

Immersed in warm Smirnoff flowering from hands.

A narrative as crooked as the branches of a Judas tree.

Fractured in the dry riverbed of names.

Essays & Poems

SANTA ROSA

Bryan Price

Toad's real name was Shannon I don't think I'm making this up but some years later (around 1996) Michael brought her to our apartment with a box of amyl nitrite that she spilled on the pillows two nights later the furniture store across the street burned to the ground we all went outside to watch and I never felt so much a part of a community—this was before everything descended into subatomic weirdness whenever I got depressed I would walk to Huntington Park to smoke cigarettes in the shadow of Grace Cathedral and try to predict who would commit suicide with a rope or belt and who might treat my body like a piece of human scrap to be picked up and flown away with

YESTERDAY

Ms.AyeVee

Yesterday was Thanksgiving & I'm thinking about you.
I mean, I'm always thinking about you
but yesterday was always your day.
Always the sound of your laughter echoing from the kitchen.
The clinks & clangs from pots & pans.
Your hands moving from one to the other, seamlessly.
Like playing conga drums, a culinary Sheila E.

Grandma,
Is a holiday still a holiday without a family to share it with?
I feel like an orphan.
Trying to find my way through the crowd but you're no longer
    here to hold my hand.
Sometimes I feel like I may never find my way.
Running around in circles.
I always seem to find myself in the exact same emotional space.
I'm lost without you.
I drop breadcrumbs as I wander through the world aimlessly.
Hoping that somehow it will be you that comes to find me.
Friends hold me as I cry for what could no longer be.
They try to help me find some morsel of happy.
Invites to parties.
Introduce me to their whole family.
Silently, I scan the room energetically looking for the person that
feels the most like you.
Talking to strangers about anything & everything just like we used to do.
I close my eyes for a second & pretend it's you.
I smile.
A ghost of gratitude.

Essays & Poems

Grandma,
I'm trying so hard to be strong like you.
I can wear your jacket but I still can't fit in your shoes.
You told me once that you wanted me to be better than you.
Have a better life.
Be a better person.
So maybe, this journey isn't about me becoming you.
Maybe it's about me becoming me & learning to walk in my own shoes.

The Book of Life After Death

MY MOTHER, THE WITCH

Courtney Harler

What I remember is your hair—too long. Stringy in the end, but never quite gray. Maybe just one white Cruella-style streak. You liked that movie, and all the Disney. You adored *Hocus Pocus*.

You loved *The Wizard of Oz*. We watched on the couch together, me cuddled into the crook at the back of your knees, your ass my pillow for when I would fall asleep before the film finished.

We made popcorn in a big black pot back then—sputtering oil, melted butter, way too much salt. Autumn was your season, and Halloween, your element. Dad made us give out boxes of raisins.

But you hid the candy in your dresser drawers, snuck bites of chocolate until the mice arrived. They'd scritch too much in the night, and you'd have to trash your stash before Dad found out.

These images of you—I call them now, as the leaves fall and the days darken. I'm waiting for the end of daylight savings time, for your witchy ways to work their magic in my dreams. Visit me.

Let's go trick-or-treating, one last time. You will wear your pointy hat and your velveteen cloak. I will dress as a kitty again, your forever familiar. Your sweet, pesky servant, always underfoot.

Essays & Poems

TEN-ITEM QUESTIONNAIRE
FOR MY GREAT-GRANDMOTHER
Dani Putney

Where were you born in South China?

What was your girlhood like?

Why did you pursue a career in opium farming?

When did you migrate to the Philippines?

Who was your spouse?

What was raising your daughter in Cebu like?

Did you know you had a granddaughter in America?

How did you die?

Are you real?

Are you inside me?

A FINAL RESTING PLACE

Susan Cohen

We drove through large iron gates of the cemetery and pulled into an empty parking lot. I tumbled out of the car and felt a kink in my leg as I stood up, still under the influence of jet lag from an eleven-hour flight. We came straight from the airport, but I would have preferred to have a hot shower and a glass of chilled Chardonnay before remembering my mother.

My friend asked to pay her respects. She was basking in the nostalgia of my mother sitting at her post in the kitchen, smiling, greeting her warmly and then wrapping her in her arms. She forgot about the dark days when my mother folded inside herself and slowly disappeared until she heard music from a silent radio.

My friend slammed her car door and stood still patiently, waiting for me to lead her to the gravesite. A wave of panic clenched my throat with the realization I had no idea how to find my mother's grave. I am a person who is naturally disoriented, who can't get from point A to B without some form of electronic navigation, but this municipal graveyard with all its sameness makes it impossible to be certain about the location of anything. The rolling hills that continued forever like an infinite pool of green. There were no religious symbols popping out of the earth and announcing themselves. All of the grave markers were identically shaped rectangles made of marble flush to the ground.

This non-denominational graveyard was fitting because my mother defied labels. Born into a Greek Orthodox family, she became Lutheran for her first husband and then converted to Catholicism for my father. My childhood home was mistaken for the governor's mansion, while she grew up in an apartment above the grocery store where new arrivals from Greece came for warm healing cups, coffee grind readings, and illegally home-brewed beer and wine. When I studied psychology in high school, I theorized my mother's mental instability came from her inability to be comfortable in her own skin.

Sometimes I think there is a science to happiness. If you exceed a number of degrees of freedom from your core, you will be lost forever

Essays & Poems

and won't find your way home. I read once that an Ethiopian woman slowly emerged from a cloud of depression after her psychologist recreated her village, complete with a tent and the smell of dishes she enjoyed as a child.

A spark of hope flew up into my throat when I saw a gnarled dry tree on top of a little hill that looked vaguely familiar. I waved my friend over and then grave after grave, I gently swept my sneaker to push aside the green blades of grass to read the name. My friend did the same. For a moment, my heart raced when the first three letters match, but then the last two letters were off, so I sighed and moved on to the next rectangle. It was a bizarre, metaphysical scavenger hunt. But then again, my whole relationship with my mother was like a game of hide and seek.

When she was well, she made me front and center of her life. But then there was the pain and fear of her absences when she sat stubbornly on her chair, living in a strange world beyond my reach. If I tried to ask her to invite me in, to describe what she saw and heard, she was angry with me, insisting that I could see and hear her hallucinations, because for her what she experienced weren't delusions at all, they were real.

It seemed as if our relationship was on a scale, where she went to extremes from being totally present to totally absent. On her good days, she reminded me of the wonder of our connection by reminding me that most mothers and daughters fought, but we were perfect together. I was her best friend and the sunshine in her life. For me, it was a heart wrenching brain teaser.

I wondered perhaps if we all are given an equal amount of love to share, but in the end, there are two kids of people. Those that have one-on-one relationships with all the devotion and intensity, where with all the highs and lows you can see the whole world in a single person, and those who gravitate to being surrounded by a community with a singular passion. Most of us interact both ways with the world, but I had the joy and horror of feeling I was my mother's entire world.

Perhaps as a child I took too much responsibility for the phases of her moods. Later in college, I wondered if I was an enabler of an unhealthy relationship by giving up writing for the yearbook, working on the school newspaper, and running for the cross-country team, to rush home and check on her. Feeling the duty and power of watching over her sanity.

It didn't feel as if I was getting any closer to her grave. There were hundreds of little rectangles, and the search seemed futile. I reignited the warm safe connection between us, hoping that sparks from her remains under the earth would ping me back, giving me a beacon to follow.

I was a six-year-old laying out pieces of phyllo dough on the counter, gently dabbling each sheet using a pastry brush, placing the béchamel sauce with feta cheese carefully on the end of the strip, and then folding it like a flag to form a perfect triangle. The sweet smell of pastry baking in the oven filled the house. My teeth sank into a small warm packet of salty cheese and creamy butter with a gentle crunch.

I busted her out of the kitchen on one cold dark winter day and brought her to the summer cottage to see the arm of the Milky Way where we made snow angels together.

Then other memories came crashing in uninvited. My mother, wearing a floppy sun hat with a pink ribbon tied under her chin, sang in Greek, swinging a piece of pepperoni pizza in the air, while the boy that sat next to me in Geometry class walked in. At that moment I wanted to be like those grave markers, indistinguishable, flush with the ground.

In the middle of the night, I was awakened by the sound of loud footsteps down the stairs, a door sliding open, and kitchen cabinet doors slamming. The house was filled with the sound of metallic clanging, and I imagined my mother was taunted by strange and angry voices accusing her of horrible thoughts or deeds, and she was being coaxed to do something that she refused, but the commands wouldn't stop. As the voices in her head became louder, she banged harder and faster, until the racket sounded like a desperate attempt to warn an ancient village of an approaching army.

I felt like I was paddling in front of a wave about to crest, knowing that I would be lifted with pieces of shells, pebbles, and grains of sand and thrown against the shore. I was nothing, nameless, and helpless merged with a chaotic blob where anything can happen.

I sat up in my bed terrified wondering how I can convince her to stop making the thunder, when I saw flashing blue and white lights on

Essays & Poems

the wall of my bedroom. I heard a pounding on the door, and a man shouting, "Police, open up!"

My friend's voice startled me.

"At this rate, it will be dark before we find her. You don't have a row number, anything? Is there anyone you can call?"

I shook my head no. Suzy Floozy, she's probably thinking. I'm still a space cadet. When I was in junior high, I lost my mittens, notebooks, and kept throwing my retainer by accident into the trash. Now as unbelievable as it seems, I even managed to lose my mother's grave. Grounded, my friend was always the one bringing me back to reality, reminding me to put on my hat and gloves, and to hurry up because my father was waiting to drive me home in his Oldsmobile with the motor running.

I spotted a shed on the crest of the hill. "Wait here," I told my friend. I came back with the coordinates scribbled on a piece of paper, from a kind retired gentlemen who takes pleasure from helping people find their loved ones. My friend relaxed, clutching the crook of my elbow to support me, anticipating the joy I would feel being reunited with my mother.

My shoulders relaxed when I recognized my father's stone that I ordered from Washington with a bronze eagle and his name and rank. My eyes scanned right, left, up, and down.

The earth around my father's stone was covered with grass, un-touched, undisturbed.

"Well, where is your mother's marker?"

I shrugged my shoulders. My tongue was heavy and lifeless.

"Are your mother's remains buried here?"

I shrugged my shoulders. What could I say? Is it possible that with the bureaucracy of death the final task to mark her final resting place was simply forgotten? Once I returned to my home halfway around the world, no one came to visit her grave, no one checked, not even once?

It's quite possible, because the only thing I am certain about my mother is that she was alone.

I couldn't recall a single unguarded conversation or warm hug be-tween my parents. My father banished himself to the basement, with his Canadian Club and the family mutt. My mother gave up a teaching career to be a housewife. There was no structure to her days. She didn't do coffee dates with girlfriends, calls from women who were witnesses to her past. Most of the time, she wandered the stacks in the library alone researching ideas that popped up in her head. She filled an entire drawer with notecards documenting the history of the potato.

She went to the neighborhood book club once but wasn't invited back after she delivered a two-hour speech that included a thorough analysis of the plot, setting, characters, point of view, figurative language, and style. Once when I saw her fading, I encouraged her to take a shower, get dressed and knock on our neighbor's door for a cup of coffee. The neighbor shut the door on her face because she said she had no patience for her.

I read somewhere that dogs need to see 20 human faces a day to be happy. I wonder sometimes if a big house, and a huge yard, and stores open 24 hours so you don't need to ask a neighbor for anything is a recipe for despair. Maybe there is a danger to having too much empty space around you.

Now, even after death, no one visited her.

I come back to the moment when my friend asks, "How are you going to fix this?"

This type of negligence is unthinkable for her, an abomination. Her family knows how to remember loved ones who have passed. Both her parents are Jewish, and they follow their customs faithfully, sitting shiva for seven days, doing a stone setting after thirty days, and then visiting the gravesite again every year. Her identity was clear and unchanging.

I reassured her. Of course, I will order my mother's stone. Of course, it's easy. I can do it from half-way around the globe. Today you can order everything on the internet. I've done it before, no big deal. I arranged for my Dad's stone to be engraved and placed on the earth. Yes, it's shocking that my mother's stone is missing.

Somehow, the stone's absence seemed shocking and fitting at the same time.

There wasn't a single stone that could pinpoint my mother's location. Her spirit was rarely at rest. She was still bouncing back and forth in waves in my brain, making me feel restless, waiting, and afraid. The fear of watching her slip between my fingers was always fresh in my

Essays & Poems

memory. She was everywhere and nowhere all at once.

Sometimes I don't know which mother to connect to, the one that is wild and unpredictable, or the one that is kind, loving, and attentive. I want to connect to both sides of her, but there is the sense of fear and love being wrapped together, shorting out the forces of attraction and repulsion. The hard part won't be ordering a stone and placing it in the earth, it will be finding a final resting place for both sides of my mother in my heart.

The Book of Life After Death

DAY AFTER DAY OF THE DEAD
Alexis Ivy

At the cemetery Panteón
General in Oaxaca City everyone
had brought marigolds
to their dead loved ones.

I visit all the gravesites
that have no marigolds —
Manuel Santiago 1956-1993
Baby Ana 1876-1879.

I count my dead — the friends
of mine who've overdosed,
and the part of me who's dead:
the one that mattered most.

I overhear a woman say
in Spanish the only time
I buy men flowers is
when they're dead.

She sweeps up after the dead
she spoke with last night.
Her cheeks red with mezcal.
She must've lost someone

she wasn't ready to lose.
I gather the skeletal
marigolds, make a bouquet.
I know there's life left in them.

Essays & Poems

HUNGRY GHOSTS FESTIVAL
Kelly Kaur

I meander through skinny corridors outside my Singapore flat
sidestep fiery burning bins filled with pungent joss sticks
salivate over plates laden with delectable offerings
of divine dumplings and bursting baos

Ah Soo kneels in front of her container, head bowed in quiet grief
uttering supplications for the lost soul of her beloved Ah Lim
relentless tears cascade onto the paper money
she passionately tosses into the fire
peering at me through smoke and haze
her haunted disembodied voice whispers

Uncle Lim is still wandering, lah
I have to give him food and money, ok
So he can live happily with other ghosts

I nod in compassion
remembering decades of muffled screams in the silent night
disguised broken bones and black eyes
shattered spirits and secret suffering

must help hungry spirit find peace in afterlife

I tenderly touch her shoulder
exorcising ghosts of pain

The Book of Life After Death

MAJOR MAGIC'S ANIMATRONIC BAND

Andrew Collard

> *Some kids send the robots fan letters. Some kids talk to them
> and even offer them slices of their pizza.*
>
> —*Detroit Free Press*, 1983

One token rattling   into Pac-Man, another lost
to the world's smallest   carousel. Some games spit
tickets good for prizes, but

> I never had enough. What did I come for, beyond
> the privilege of beginning,   token after
> token, the disembodied

voice startling   the band to clunky strumming.
On stage,   a psychedelic drum major, side-eyeing
the human-esque snare behind him,

> beating its own face, a bear   maybe borrowed
> from the Disney jamboree, an eight-foot-tall
> robotic lion, and you,

with your awkward   walrus-wobble, permanently
slouched stage left.   O Sergeant Pepperoni, gentle
and anxious, I recall you

> grasping your sax for dear life   as if to hide
> behind it, tusks   like inconvenient straws.
> Are the lights still on

where you are? Are they dim   as they were in 1983
there,   in some east-sider's basement showroom
where you mimic The Coasters

Essays & Poems

for broadcast over the internet   at the insistence
of the tipsy and middle-aged? O, to feel surprised
again, and safe. Dear friend, so far

from home, today I saw a single token   I might've held
once, good for use only   in a space long since destroyed,
sell for seven dollars on eBay,

as if it could return its buyer   to the bright red
doors, the acid-damaged storefront ringing out
like an infection, somehow,

from the plaza   you carried singlehandedly
into consequence, divorced from your big-box neighbors,
restaurants, from concepts like *rent*

and *crime*. I still can't name   which street
your old lot   swelled toward, the route a language
only drivers were permitted

to master, a secret circuit   between anywhere and back
I only recognize   by habit, now, in my second-hand
Odyssey, dribbling oil along

the corridors of the suburbs   as I trace these half-
gone signals   beneath the rising curtain of night
to their point of origin, to you —

43

HOUSE Of CARDS
Paul Skenazy

Dad was an installment dealer. He sold clothes, bedding, watches, lamps, radios, televisions, drapes, towels and pretty much anything except food to customers who could not afford to pay all at once. Instead he drove to their houses and apartments all over Chicago and picked up weekly or biweekly installments on the bill—a dollar, two, five, ten. He started working for my uncle, Dad's sister's husband, when he finished high school in 1934. My uncle bought him a Model T and in the late 1930s sold Dad a portion of his business, which he then took back and tended for my father during World War II. For fifty years, six days a week, Dad would leave the house at seven or eight in the morning and drive around the city, moving from neighborhood to neighborhood, doorway to doorway. These were poor people for the most part who lived in cramped spaces in rundown buildings. Dad climbed the two, three, four stories through dark hallways. Or sometimes through alleys or tunnels that led to basement doors or wooden stairways and back porches crammed with refrigerators, bicycles and clothes hanging on lines stretched across from one apartment to the next. He drove more than 30,000 miles a year without ever leaving the city limits. I don't know how many miles he walked and climbed.

I never could figure out how to describe what Dad did to friends. "A salesman," I'd say. "What does he sell—Condoms? Cars?" "Towels, clothes, radios, TVs." "Like appliances? Washers and driers?" "Household things: blenders, waffle irons, electric fry pans. Sheets, drapes." I would explain how my dad couldn't tell reds from grays, how even traffic lights baffled him except for the relative position of the red, yellow, and green. How they wouldn't take him in the Army Air Force when he tried to enlist because he failed the color blindness test, so he wound up in the Signal Corps instead. Yet chose clothes for hundreds of men and women every year, not to mention me until I had some say in what I wore.

Installment dealers kept records of their customers on account cards. The cards were a beige that darkened with the years. They

Essays & Poems

sat alongside him on the front seat of his car. They said "Roosevelt Budget Co" across the top, though there was no "Co," since Dad was the business. There was a line for the customer's name, and alongside that the names of a husband or wife and kids; the address; the phone number—the numbers often crossed out and replaced by a second or third if the customer moved, or were one of his oldest. The cards were three or four inches across, ten inches lengthwise, four columns: space for a descriptive entry, a date, a payment amount, a running tab. My father would note a purchase across the width of the left column. He would also add notes to himself about what he needed to buy for someone, say to someone. The notes went on torn scraps of white paper clipped to the top of a card so he had them when he got to the customer's house. Some of the older customers had two, three, four, even six cards; one active, the others archived in a rusty metal storage unit that lived in our basement. Newer customers had just a few entries on theirs, the beige card pale, clean, the edges sharp and not crumbling from years in and out of his hands.

Usually questions about Dad's work ended with me saying he was an old-fashioned credit card and catalogue: you told him what you wanted, he picked it out, brought it to you, you paid him in installments. He offered installments more than merchandise. His work was clear to me, growing up watching him each night, working for him from the time he let me when I hit my senior year of high school. Everyone I grew up with sold something: Dad's buddy Dave owned a dry cleaner's; my Uncle Max sold furniture; Uncle Abe sold cameras; Dad's three sisters were married to three other installment dealers. My friend Mike's dad was a butcher, my friend Dave's mom ran the knitting store where my aunts went every Saturday to buy their skeins and sit and knit with her for a morning. But it didn't translate, this kind of work, once I got to college, where my friends came from houses in the suburbs, parents who were doctors and lawyers, worked downtown in Chicago offices, had college degrees. So I stopped talking about it.

At five or six p.m. when my father got home he would sort his cards. His card file was an old cardboard shoe box that he kept in the cabinet below his desk along with his adding machine, his account books, and printed stationary that read "Roosevelt Budget Co. / 555 West Roosevelt Road / Chicago, Illinois 60607" at the top of each sheet. Before

45

The Book of Life After Death

we moved to our house in 1953, we lived in a four room apartment and Dad's desk was the formica kitchen table, a bean-shaped thing with an aqua paisley design on the top, a metallic border, and metal cylindrical legs. When we moved to our house Dad worked at the dining room table, polished walnut though always covered with a thick protective pad. Eventually we added a den and he finally had his own desk: a small thing, about a third the width and half the depth of where I type this. Closed, it looked like a drawer; it folded down, then slid outward slightly, revealing a white working surface and six cubbyholes. He sat on a metal card chair with a vinyl seat that he kept folded in the den closet.

The "Roosevelt" in "Roosevelt Budget" came from Roosevelt Road, running East to West at 1200 South in Chicago. The area has been rebuilt. The University of Illinois, Chicago Circle campus covers a neighborhood that once housed huge outdoor markets of stalls that went up early each morning, came down each night. This was the famous Hull House area, populated from the early twentieth century by immigrant communities: Italians, Poles, Greeks, Germans, Jews from all over the Mediterranean. It was where my father grew up. At home we called Roosevelt "The Street," as in, "Dad's working late tonight on The Street." "Tell him Dad's meeting a customer on The Street at 3:30 if he wants to find him."

After the open market days came buildings. Dad's first office on The Street that I remember was in a converted bank. The downstairs was filled with stalls, like an indoor flea market, each stall a separate business—people selling women's or men's clothes, canned goods, fresh fish and meat, salamis, bread. Upstairs a balcony ran around the perimeter, with cubbyholes created by thin plywood where the installment dealers worked. Dad's office had a large metal desk, a thin door with a lock, and a metal file cabinet.

Settled at his desk at home, my father would turn over one card after another. Most of the customers paid in cash, a few by check. How much depended on how often they missed a payment, the time he knew them, how much they owed. He'd write the day's take in a neat column on a scratchpad, then check his figures with an old hand calculator that he cranked each time he added a notation. He'd compare that figure with the cash in his pocket. He carried around $200-

46

Essays & Poems

250 to start a day, most of it in small bills for change. He'd deduct the amount he started with from his new total—on a Saturday, often well over two thousand dollars—then reconcile that with his list of figures; if they didn't jive, he'd return to the cards, checking them again. This was as close as he ever came to his high school dream of being a CPA. When his cash flow and figures balanced, the cards for the day were divided, those on a weekly route into one pile, the bi-weekly customers in another. He wrapped the groups of cards in thick rubber bands, then dropped them into the shoebox, which had dividers cut from file folders labeled Monday through Saturday. The cash went into another thick rubber band for deposit at the bank.

When my father died I lost 40 pounds in a month. I had nightmares. I wanted to go to a movie, a baseball game. My father reached in his pocket for money but didn't have any. My father, who always carried a folded hundred dollar bill in his wallet among the family photos; who bought gold Kruggerands he kept in a safe deposit box. I couldn't sleep. I listened to NPR news broadcasts. I spent hours in bed tuned to talk radio absorbing insufferable right-wing arguments. A friend told me she lived through pain with the help of Bach's "Goldberg Variations," so I tried Glenn Gould at 3, 4, 5 a.m. I woke at 7 to prepare lunch bags for my three children, draw funny faces on the bags, get my kids to school; I roused myself later each day to pick them up and drive to soccer games and karate lessons. One night I asked my ex- to come hold me in her arms for twenty minutes while I cried. Another night I took the kids downtown to a film, parked the car in the city lot. When I came out, the front window was full of shit. There was a diaper plastered to the passenger side. I stood there and cried. For three or four minutes I think, long enough for the kids to come out, stand next to me and rub up and down my arms. I stopped, got the kids back into the car, turned on the wipers and window spray, used the diaper to sop up what shit didn't come off with the water.

Eventually, the bank building was demolished. The people who owned the stalls found an empty lot on Roosevelt Road and built a tiny mall, with a guard post at the entry so you had to be cleared to come in and park. The stores were supposed to be strictly wholesale, only sell-

The Book of Life After Death

ing to the installment dealers and their customers, but that didn't last long. Most of the business still came through the dealers, though, who had a separate building with offices that were only slightly larger than the plywood cubicles in the old bank building. Independent Clothing Co., Associated Clothing, United Appliance: anonymous names. Dad reserved a couple hours each day to work on The Street picking up merchandise, meeting friends over lunch, schmoozing, playing cards when he had the time, calling customers. Dad hated selling but he loved to talk to people. People he knew, he felt comfortable with; when I started bringing college friends over, he was nervous, seemed to feel out of his depth, though he hid his uncertainties with affability. He hated going places he didn't know, stuck to the same restaurants and bowling alleys, golf courses and stores all his life. If it hadn't been for Mom and the chance to spend vacations with couples he loved, I doubt he would ever have traveled.

When I realized I wanted to kill myself, I started on antidepressants— one a.m. and one p.m. I started seeing a healer. She led me through visions of past lives—Egyptian, Victorian. I was a peasant, a worker. I saw myself walking slowly down an endless highway in a flat dry plain, weighed down by suitcases of parental grief and accusation. "Let them go," she told me. "Leave them along the roadside." I didn't believe a word and hung on to every one. I tried tai chi with a corporate guru and life coach who traded me lessons in movement for my help with a book he wanted to write on Mastery and Power. I remember the jasmine tea we'd drink. He told me tales of wandering through multiple healing systems to discover what worked for him.

Because his desk did not slide out very far, and Dad was six foot two, there was not enough room for his knees to fit straight under. So he was always turned a bit one way or the other, usually towards the TV in the corner, which was more or less always on. Walter Cronkite with national news just before dinner. Sports if he could find it: the Cubs played no night games then, White Sox night games weren't broadcast, no national games either until World Series time each year, and those too were during the day. Saturdays had college football and Sundays the pros. No ESPN.

Essays & Poems

I started working for my dad on Saturdays in high school. When I went off to college I lived at the other end of Chicago: 5500 South, vs. our house at 5700 North. That meant fourteen miles across the width of the city, and about four miles east to west. I had a job on campus renting televisions in the university hospital. I'd call in each day at three to get a list of the new rentals. I'd go to the storeroom, find the 19" black-and-white portables on their metal stands, plug them in to be sure they worked, ride the elevators, have the patients sign for the sets, do my best to get a decent picture with the rabbit ears, and then wander the halls getting renewals from other patients, or picking up sets from empty rooms. Sometimes someone would die— "expire," the nurses called it, as if it were a magazine subscription. I'd find the bed empty, the mattress rolled up on the metal box springs, the TV waiting for me. I would walk home with a few hundred dollars in my pockets late at night, often in the middle of the quiet streets to avoid rubbing shoulders with anyone else out at that hour. I'd come home for weekends once a month, he'd hand me my pile of installment cards arranged in a route to travel from one stop to the next. I'd borrow his car at night to see friends, then head back to the university the next morning on the El so I could finish my school work. I got to know my way around the streets, apartment buildings, the smells of the neighborhoods. I learned to be comfortable with some of the customers, though I never liked trying to sell them something. I also was embarrassed by what he did, or how what he did supported me, while I picketed against the war in Vietnam, claimed allegiance with the Black protests all over the North and South, discovered James Baldwin's essays about Jewish merchants in Black neighborhoods. And I cried each time he let me off at the El to head back to my dorm room, hugged me to him, rubbed his abrasive cheek against mine.

When his customers were not at home, or did not pay, my father phoned them. While my sister and I set the table and mom cooked, or just after we ate while we started the dishes, he was on the phone complaining about a missed payment, working to nail down a promise about when he could come by for the cash. Or he would raise his voice and threaten to turn the account over to a collection agency. Frequently he would say he had to check with his boss before he could agree to the proposed terms—a boss who didn't exist, but made it easier

49

for him to pretend sympathy, one worker to another. After dinner, he would return to his desk to plan his next day's route through the city in front of sitcoms and quiz shows and sleuths: *Father Knows Best, The $64,000 Question, The Rockford Files*. My mother usually sat with him, darning clothes, rifling through magazines, folding socks. Dad would pull out his cards from his shoebox, unloop the rubber band from the accounts, and imagine his next day—when he might find people home, who he needed to meet when. He'd calculate the one-way streets, the traffic flows that altered with predictable regularity. He spent his days in more and more comfortable GM cars: Chevvies, then Buicks, finally Cadillacs. When he started making more money, he bought a new one every two years.

There are no more installment dealers. They have been replaced by credit cards and no money down offers from furniture and appliance stores. The business lasted from the end of urban street markets to the fall of Vietnam. It kept me and all my uncles and aunts, cousins and their children, in food. It taught me how to navigate Chicago streets and what work was. I keep a few of my father's cards in a shoebox along with his letter opener and fountain pen.

Essays & Poems

GREENHOUSE GHOSTS

Chloe Biggs

I am the greenhouse that no one comes to visit anymore.
The Victorian language of the flowers does not escape me,
but no one else has spoken it in over a hundred years.
I am dramatic, introspective, neurotic.
The tea I steep is always too strong,
and tastes bitter to those who
enjoy psychological balance.

I am the greenhouse that grows only dead things.
No one comes looking
for the types of flora
that creep along my sills and crowd against my walls
and push and push and push until
a branch cracks the glass.
Don't bother to run.
They cannot slither around anyone's ankles
but mine.
I water and sing to and tend to
a nursery full of ghosts.

I sit for long spells in this house of windows that
I have created,
feeling that I have lived enough to cultivate
the phantoms and tender torment of
someone five times my age.
Won't you savor them with me for a moment?
My ghosts do not wrap themselves
in cellophane and luxurious ribbons.
I never did find a pair of shears
that could tame them.
They'll strangle each other
before I find a way
to cut them down.

The Book of Life After Death

WITH ARTHUR AFTER THE MEMORIAL
FOR HIS WIFE

Xiaoly Li

This is the squirrels' dining table,
he points to a stone bench where
many hickory husks are broken open.

> I smile at him as I walk
> in the well-cut grass
> dividing his acres of hill land.

Have you thought of what you want
to do before you die?
Just do it now. You never know
when it's coming.

He looks at me keenly, next to a cross
where his last horse is buried.

> *I write poetry and meditate to see*
> *what is real,* my mouth a little dry.

Do you think you will be happier once
you know what is real?

> A hazy sky I can't see through.

Barbara and I even talked about
sailing the Pacific
all the way to China.

> A white dove flies by.

Sea sets us free.

> We walk into the barn where we used
> to play pool. Everything is orderly
> arranged and clean.

Essays & Poems

I see his exercise chair.

Are you still lifting weights?

*Of course! You think I should sit here
doing nothing?* he slouches his shoulders
as if he's an old weak man, then laughs.
The edge of his sorrow softens more.

*How do you maintain everything
so well? That is a lot of work.*

*You call this work? It is gold.
You just clean it so it shines again.*

The Book of Life After Death

RETIREMENT

C. Prudence Arceneaux

I don't believe in God, the Father Almighty.
I do wonder where my father is right now.

Today, the sky, Maximum Blue, colored with a five-year-old's
missed strokes, the starling in the bushes shouts—then growls—a bee
surprised by its wing.
                                        I'm weeding. Again.
I want to believe it will stop, but even in drought,
they punch up. Defeated, I stretch my back and remember
my father's pleasure at this task, his body long as my shadow,
hunched to the dirt. I wonder if he found a job there—where there is.

If when he showed up, he said, "Put me to work."
If he tends gardens, if they have gardens.
If he puts in a full day's work, an hour for lunch,
if he "lazy asses" at the others who sit in that otherly light.
If he turns from his dark words to his bear-like hands
and gently covers a new seed.
If he needs to do this to think he deserves a rest.

Essays & Poems

CONSIDERATION Of BURIAL

Flynn Dexter

I would like to visit you
At your grave
Lay something living
On this heavy;

To watch the flowers wilt
Is watching your decline
Again
And again.

But the flowers
Had no choice.

It is hard,
Sitting in peace
With so much
Muffled density
Between me
And your laughter.

How comforting
To know
The people who love you
Can find you,
Talk to you,
Without asking your mother
Shamefully.

Did you know that anyone can call
To ask where you are buried?

How bittersweet —
To know that there is only one way
To close
The gap between us.

THE FLINCH FACTOR

Rebecca Douglas

It's the one thing you can't Google: How to write an epitaph for an abusive parent. I know, I tried.

My mother was dead and at 40, I had a headstone to arrange. As an only child—father absent, then dead years before—the task fell to me to select the material and the message. I was to email my chosen wording to the memorial company.

I'd been assaulted by a well-meaning brochure, full of chunks of granite and marble etched into eternity. Every example said 'In loving memory of' and cited the deceased as the 'Beloved son of…' or 'Loving and caring mother of…'. I was at a loss. Where were the engravings for the 'Barely tolerated' and 'Outright despised'?

The only specimens Google could come up with that strayed from the tried-and-true loving/beloved formula were the jokers from beyond the grave. Funnily enough, I didn't feel like laughing it up in the fashion of Mel Blanc's 'That's all folks' memorial or Leslie Nielsen's 'Let 'er rip'.

It's not something one can bring up in polite company either—then you run the risk of inflicting the flinch or rather, having it inflicted upon you. It's a momentary movement, the hint of disgust quickly ushered into a quiet corner, but not before you notice.

But I flinch too. Your alien family, with parents who never screamed threats at each other on the front stoop, who haven't yelled at you for applying to university, who didn't sabotage your every attempt at a normal life because they were afraid to be alone. How could you grow up in an environment so lacking?

It's not right, it won't last, it'll all shatter once you get too comfortable. You'll see.

Except it doesn't. The illusion doesn't shatter because it's not an illusion. Comfort and stability can always be relied upon, until I drop the unsettling knowledge on you that not everyone's family is like that. You've read about it, of course, but you don't want it laid out right in front of you.

Essays & Poems

So you flinch, even when you've invited me to tell you about my abnormal family. You've asked questions, but only some answers are acceptable. The ones like yours. It's a trap — I'm not just randomly volunteering upsetting information because I like making things awkward, but it's still my fault if I do. It makes you uncomfortable to hear the truth. So my choices are either to lie, or joke, or change the subject. To cover and conceal.

Childhood trauma survivors are supposed to bear the weight of the hurt itself and the lifetime of carrying the secret, but others can't even bear the weight of being told. So it's thrown back in your face, slammed back in its box, and you think even harder before letting those demons out again.

Why don't victims say something earlier? Chances are they've tried, but even well-meaning listeners flinch and then deny — How can you say that about your mother? But they're faaaaaaaaaaamily. Life's too short to hold grudges. You only get one mum. You'll be sorry when they're gone.

Except I'm not sorry. I feel like breaking out the confetti. My mourning is only for me and my life of solitary suffering. Selfish, no? At least I matter to someone, though. Just not her, and never did. But I must pretend cuddles and caring were there, for the sake of others who can't bear to see the world as it really is, or ever was. The 'Loving' before 'mother of' a mandatory fairytale to be carved in stone, dishonouring my pain and my experience.

And so I sigh, and I put it in, and I take it out, and I wonder what's allowed.

The Book of Life After Death

DISCO BALLS & fRANK SINATRA

Audrey Forbes

Inside the Italian restaurant that I've worked at for less than a year
   I hear his name like stale bread moments in the back house
        O, how I have harbored this memory
                how I have quelled this closing
                how I have tried to wrap it into tablecloths
            fold it neatly into fancy napkins
   his name like a customer
          minutes before I shut down the podium
          "I can take you," I say.
   Because I ought to. There must be space somewhere —
& so I find a table right under the quiet disco light.

Essays & Poems

ELEGY FOR A GAMBLER

Jen Karetnick

If it is true that "the dead have all the glory of the world,"[1] then so too do the missing, the lost, the stolen, the runaways, the mentally absent, the Krissy Houstons and Lamar Odoms found with lungs like water balloons, induced into comas with legal drugs, only one of them lucky enough to survive the race back into a society that will no longer offer garlands of roses because "we live... in feelings, not in figures on a dial."[2] Yet Amber and Silver alerts buzz our phones like low-flying planes with messages begging us to look, implore us to be witnesses, take note, as if in this particular age we are actually more aware of the world around us rather than less, only glancing up from gadgets to avoid walking through glass and into door jambs or knocking our foreheads against the woodpecker-splintered poles supporting these essential wires.

But the first time the unheard-of happens, no such warnings exist, so when the fifty flamingo chicks were snatched from Hialeah Park Race Track one July to be resold on the exotic pet market, "a very profitable thing to be involved in if you're a thief,"[3] no Rose or Rouge or Fuchsia alerts were delivered mobile to our inauthentic eyes and ears. No images of birds adorable with fuzz that stood out as if rubbed against rubber to create static electricity were sent for biometric identification. No *If you see this flamingo, please contact...* And perhaps there won't be a next time for this flock who, like so many citizens of this portmanteau city, *exilios* of Cuba, have planted their genetic code in such uncertain, urban earth, once considered by the natives a "pretty prairie,"[4] for generations now. When giving birth is the original gamble, keeping offspring from harm is merely a show parlay: whatever one gets, they all get. But the thief—he is the first gambler. And he can take many forms: Bird wrangler, horse track regular, poker player, brother.

My brother taught me to gamble with pennies on the floor of the den where cave crickets exercised their moon-landing legs the same year the Meadowlands Racetrack was born, the year of his Bar Mitzvah,

The Book of Life After Death

the year he quit Judaism, the year my parents brought home the Siberian Husky pup he trained to attack and drag me down the stairs by my ankles as if hauling a live crow through snow drifts. Even though he cheated, always claiming the deal, labeling himself the house, I loved my brother enough back then to let him fleece me of my piggy-bank savings the way a farmer sticks his hand under a nesting hen for her eggs: I hardly squawked. Learning to play Blackjack, Texas Hold 'Em, Seven Card Stud—these were my own diversionary tactics. Of course they didn't work in the long term; a wager never does pay off that way. For those of us who give too much, there will always be recipients who want nothing in the end. The shared account, bloated by the drop and release of ridged, deliberate coins, waits. This time, when the alert sounds, it's in code, a terse range of monophonic blues that calls all our bets, and never again allows for a raise.

[1] From the poem "We live in deeds, not years; in thoughts, not breaths" by Philip James Bailey

[2] From the poem "We live in deeds, not years; in thoughts, not breaths" by Philip James Bailey

[3] Jorge Pino, the Florida Fish and Wildlife Conservation Commission

[4] Hialeah comes from the Muskogee words *haiyakpo* (prairie) and *hili* (pretty)

Essays & Poems

REASONS WHY GHOSTS EXIST

Arthur Kayzakian

Because cobwebs were the ancient band-aids for wounds.
Because the web is rich in vitamin k, the webicillin stops the body
    from leaking.
Because a woman in Paris lost her wedding ring in 1972 and then
    found it on the gravestone of her second husband in 2021.
Because curtains in the backdrop of an empty room.
Because take me with you.
Because light invades but acts like we should be grateful for its arrival.
Because blood. Because blood donors receive a text from an unknown
    number, each time blood is used. The message reads: thank you 00000.
Because men who cut down trees end up in a wooden box.
Because laughter is found on a tape recorder every 1.7 seconds.
Because we will never know who loves us.
Because we may know who loves us but never know how much.
Because the West says "love yourself" and it feels like living with a
    stranger.
Because it would take 60 minutes to drive to space.
Because we are still searching for a boulevard to the sky.
Because clouds. Because flies. Because elevators.
Because my hand moves faster than my shame.
Because I heard my parents separate through the wall of my room.
Because covid was the light that took my cousin.
Because a spider bit my left hand when I was six.
Because the shortest wars are the ones where we make love.
Because now I hear footsteps on the wooden floor in my den in the
    rhythm of my cousin's walk.
Because the spider bite itches at every funeral.
Because money. Because tree.
Because money is a dead tree.
Because trees fly in reverse when we dream.
Because a flock of ravens is misinterpreted as conspiracy.
Because the smell of borsht drifts through the slim crack of a door
    half open.

The Book of Life After Death

Because my cousin is the second husband of a woman with a missing ring.
Because air is jealous of the way you hover.
Because vapor. Because the steam from chopped onions spices the eye.
The minted leaves and butter sliding off a slab of lamb at the speed of
    smoke.
Because memory. The potent tinge of coal after a fire dies.
Because money is the dead tree that split my parents.
Because a spider bite is a small phantom made for the hand.
Like a cousin who never returns but lingers in a dream.
Like a missing wedding ring burning around my finger.

Essays & Poems

I'M TIRED OF KILLING YOU

Hunter Hazelton

If you came home, I could show you
how to fit a lifetime in a cabinet.

How easy it was for your time to pass.
Encumbering me with these tokens

and riddles: the photos that stop you in age,
scribbled-on notepads telling me again

of promises not kept. I cannot bear
to stuff another found memory

in the shoebox.

If you came home, I'd say take it, take it all back:
the moth-eaten trench we bought in Italy,

the Spotify playlist I cannot delete, the street
I can no longer drive. But you can't.

Don't tell me otherwise.
I do not want your totems

nor mementos. I want the drawer
to be a drawer, for another

bedframe to saw in half, so I don't
have to remember anymore.

The trunk of clothes meant for Goodwill
mocks me, says, You poor, sad boy,

63

The Book of Life After Death

don't you know he's gone?
I'll put you in the wardrobe

And you'll be somewhere else —
Somewhere unreachable.

Come through the door and you're home.
Come through the door and say nothing.

You won't anyway. Throw the photos away
And I'm terrible. Throw them in the drawer

And it's another grief to open later.
Another burden in the bureau.

What am I going to do
With your shoes? Perhaps

One day you'll need them. Perhaps
One day you'll finally walk away.

Essays & Poems

A CRAFT TALK

Colin Pope

So this guy, this asshole, he comes into room 409 and sits down on the little floral-pattern couch and talks to our class about the poems he's writing. They're about his brother's suicide, how his brother jumped off the Golden Gate bridge three years ago. "The Golden Gate is notorious in the suicide community," he says. "Suicidologists call it a 'suicide magnet.'"

I'm in the second year of my poetry MFA and my girlfriend, Jennie, has just hanged herself, three months before this joker shows up. He's passing through, on his way from one someplace to another someplace, and he's deigned to come speak to us about his suicide poems for a day. It's likely that he was invited by the faculty to "help the program heal" or some bullshit, but nobody ever tells us why he's there. His name is Jeff, of course.

"The Golden Gate is the most jumped-off bridge in America," Jeff says, really laying it on, really rubbing in everyone's faces how much he's studied suicide.

My first reaction is to yell at him and tell him that studying won't help and that he's the stupidest person who ever loved anyone who committed suicide if he thinks it will. But I don't. I sit in my chair and squint at him as he preaches at us under the fluorescent lights of the classroom.

When I was in undergrad, a decade before I met Jennie, I listened to the professor tell my Intro to Creative Writing class the story about Sylvia Plath's suicide. Plath set a final breakfast of milk and bread outside her children's bedroom door, then sealed them in with duct tape and rolled towels. Then she went to the kitchen, turned on her gas oven, stuck her head inside, and breathed deep. It took her about seven minutes to die.

"One thing you can say about poets," my professor said. "We have the highest rate of them all." He was a rotund, ruddy-faced guy, and he sounded proud.

The Book of Life After Death

Some student, some jerk said, "Well, what about dentists?"

"Who cares about dentists?" the professor said. We all laughed, then went back to workshopping our angsty, oversexed teenage poetry.

Jennie lived alone in a house on a small ranch on the outskirts of town. She rented the place from a local farmer who let his animals roam all over the property. Pulling up the dirt drive to Jennie's house, it wasn't uncommon to find her communing with a horse or donkey in the front yard, feeding it out of her palm or making clumsy attempts to climb up and ride. She was never successful.

One day, we were in her kitchen after a class, eating tortilla chips. We were always eating tortilla chips in that kitchen, standing around the center island and figuring ourselves out.

"So what is postmodernism then, really?" I asked her. She was much smarter than me and had read all that critical theory.

"It's just made up," she said, munching. "It's something people made up when they forgot how to love one another."

"You mean, after the war?" I asked her. In our class that day, we'd spent a lot of time talking about Wallace Stevens, William Carlos Williams, and what happened after modernism, after World War I.

"No, just in general. Like any time artists want to examine why they can't feel their own emotions, it's postmodern. Like, signifier, signified, all that shit. I mean, who cares about semiotics when you're trying to tell someone you fucking love them?"

I nodded my head, only vaguely aware of the things she spoke about. Our relationship lasted just over a year, and the whole time I was determined to conceal how ignorant I was. So I nodded a lot, said "uh huh."

"You just can't really put a label on how you feel, ya know? Emotions are instantaneous. They just exist. That's why real, true poetry is so important. Because sound is meaning beyond intent."

Jennie had named the donkey Harriet, and just then we heard it laugh from somewhere out on the yard. When Harriet brayed, it sounded like a series of wheezy guffaws.

"Exactly," Jennie said, nodding her head solemnly. "Exactly."

Jeff leans back on the little floral couch, lounging, really showing us how relaxed he is as he continues his discourse on his brother's suicide.

"Of course, more men commit suicide than women," Jeff tells us, his slender legs crossed that way that skinny people can cross them, completely overlaid.

"Oh yeah?" I say. "Oh fucking yeah, Jeffy? I guess that means you win suicide. I guess that means you're the fucking emperor of useless statistics. I hope you read so much about suicide that your brother comes back, I really do, I hope he just comes waltzing right out of the fucking Pacific like a mermaid. Isn't that how it works? You just keep reading, Jeff, and your precious brother will undie and you can get your fucking doctorate in necromancy. Sound good, fucker?"

I don't say that, though. Instead, I sit there trying to figure out how he can do research on suicide without feeling like someone's stomping on his stomach. How he can turn his brother—his own brother—into a statistic, like he was just some guy who jumped off a bridge in California.

The police seized Jennie's suicide note before I could see it, but I later learned that it contained two lines by Rilke. They're from his *Book of Hours: Love Poems to God*:

*You run like a herd of luminous deer
and I am dark, I am forest.*

This is a pretty concise summary of Jennie's relationship to the world. We didn't speak too much about God, but she was definitely attuned to the spirituality of nature. The forest, the deer, the light, and the expression of these soul connections in a poem are all accurate.

That these lines mean something beyond the intellectual, that deconstructing them or dissecting them won't help you understand their underlying meaning, this is what's important. They are whole, like the natural world. One can theorize about the atoms that compose a block of wood or a deer, but in the end the atoms don't matter because the skin is relieved by its contact with wood, the heart leaps with each weightless bound of the deer. We need only believe what we feel.

Relying on emotion is the most human choice, and it's all one really need know about Jennie. I could tell you that she was tall and slender, that she kept six ducks and three chickens at the ranch, that I fell in love with her the first time I saw her standing in the kitchen of the Katherine Anne Porter House during the pre-semester mixer before our first year of the MFA. I could tell you I was grateful for her, that she was "too beautiful for this world."

But really, the best explanation of Jennie is that she rooted herself in her own feelings. It would've been unimaginable for her to act against them. What this means, then, is that she made her last choice with both eyes open. She chose not to feel.

"But why would men do it more often?" some idiot asks. Jeff looks up at the ceiling with one of those smirky, quizzical expressions, like he really has to think about that one, like it's a real humdinger.

"Lots of reasons," Jeff says. "Women's ability to communicate emotions. The ability to ask for help. But what's strange is women outnumber men in suicide *attempts* by about two to one."

Everyone nods their heads and mumbles to one another and Jeff, the fucking genius, isn't even trying to suppress his grin anymore. He's proud that his brother's death led him to such a wealth of knowledge so that now, now he can be the center of attention. His brother's death is really paying off now, and it's hard for him to keep from smiling.

My fists are literally balled, my knuckles turning white. I think of my Jennie, how I picked up a cardboard box of her ashes and transported them from the funeral parlor to her mother's hands, how I offered her mother a box about the size of a photo album and inside that box was her daughter, the person I used to kiss.

"Let's pause our discussion for a minute and I'll read a poem that looks at some of these gender politics," Jeff says. "I think it'll be helpful."

I'm almost out of body. I'm so enraged I can almost see myself as I sit in the graduate seminar room in Flowers Hall, that ghastly light raining down, Jeff's experimental, academic verse pounding me over the head so hard I have to clench my eyes shut to keep them from bursting.

I didn't learn about John Berryman, really, until I was in a "Problems

Essays & Poems

in Language and Literature" class my first year of the MFA. I'd picked up his collected poems at a Barnes & Noble when I lived in New York, but I'd pretty much just read the same few "Dream Songs," the good ones, and ignored the rest until I went to school.

"He pushed persona beyond the bounds of modernism," the professor, an aging white guy, said. "He was one of the first postmodern poets."

"So does that mean he was a liar?" someone asked.

"No, of course not," the professor said. "He just invented his own way to tell a different truth."

"Sounds like bullshit," the student said. We all laughed. Jennie was in that class too, and she giggled and snorted. Her whole face brightened when she smiled, and her snorting made everyone else laugh the more. She was adorable like that, and she tossed her long brown hair forward and tried to hide her face in embarrassment.

Doing research for a half-assed class presentation, I learned Berryman jumped off a bridge in Minneapolis. Postmodern or not, he couldn't quite get his aim right and ended up landing in a silty mudbar on the riverside below. He was found the next morning, asphyxiated by mud.

"Does anyone have any questions?" Jeff asks after he's finished reading. He's the suicide-expert poet and the rest of the class, many of whom vaguely knew Jennie, we're just stupid onlookers at the death fair.

Nobody asks anything. In point of fact, it would be nearly impossible to pose any questions about the nonsensical babble he's just read. Jeff's is not the type of poetry meant to be read aloud or, frankly, to be understood. It's that type of poetry wherein the poet believes himself a brilliant man and the rest of us are expected to delve deeply into the possible meanings of each overwrought line and pause.

When the silence grows uncomfortably awkward, someone finally asks, "What's the name of the book you're working on?"

"It's called *Riven, the Light Treatise*," he says with a straight face. I start laughing. Nobody else joins in, though, and I stop and look around and I see that these people honestly think this is a good title for a book of poems supposedly based upon the poet's brother's suicide.

69

This is the topper, the absolute limit. After I've sat in this room for ninety minutes, listening to Jeff's unfeeling, pretentious, impersonal gobbledygook, he has the audacity to say *Riven, the Light Treatise*. It's so bad it makes me queasy.

"Alright, that's it. I'm going to the bathroom," I say. I really say this, out loud, as I stand up.

I clomp around the halls for a few minutes, my fury waning, and then I start feeling sort of sad for Jeff and his brother. They're both far away from each other's realities, and as such Jeff has miscalculated and floated away from the immensity of the loss. The grief over his brother's death doesn't appear to have made the slightest dent in the riverbanks of Jeff's heart, and instead he's studied suicidology and psychology to sieve away the filth of his own pain. So it seems now, at the end of knowledge, his brother's death is just a fact of Jeff's life, like a statistic or a date or a name scrawled in an address book.

Through studying poetry, I've accidentally learned about dozens of famous poet suicides. There's Hart Crane, of course, who leapt off the back of a cruiseliner when he was returning from Mexico. Anne Sexton in her car, in her garage. Paul Celan supposedly flopped into the Seine River and was found days later by wayward fishermen.

There's such a thing as "the Sylvia Plath effect," which dictates that poets are more prone to mental illness than other types of writers and artists. This is true. A psychologist did a survey of poets and the results showed a higher tendency towards depression and mood disorders, particularly among female poets.

To be clear, I didn't learn about the Sylvia Plath effect via research. Someone told me about the study after Jennie died and then I tried my best to ignore its existence. Such things are difficult to ignore, however, since the mind hunts for pockets in which to place understanding.

Strangely, it ended up comforting me to think Jennie's suicide was of a statistical probability, like it was preordained. By some cosmic magic, the dice had been rolled years before I'd ever met her and her numbers simply came up wrong. She was a female poet. As such, I felt more like an unlucky bystander, simply marking the ebb of poetry's black tide which, for whatever reason, swept her out to sea with the

Essays & Poems

rest of them.

Nothing much happened when I returned to room 409. Jeff had finished his "craft talk" and was mincing around with the students, posturing and swooning over shared affinities for certain books and poets.

It would be a much more entertaining story if I said I walked into the room and punched him right in the mouth or spat in his eye, but I didn't. I just felt bad for him. It was too easy to cast my anger at the living, at Jeff and my teachers and even my classmates. A lot of people in the workshop knew Jennie, and I felt a strange admixture of anger and pity toward them for sitting docilely through Jeff's little talk along with me. Instead of confronting anyone, I watched from afar as Jeff niggled over the importance of certain writers, as he bowed his head and gesticulated and gave out his email address to some of the students.

Jeff didn't know anything more or less than anyone else. He was hiding inside science for the same reasons that any other dumb animal crawls away to hide when it's injured. Though the trees were highfalutin in his case, it was still a sort of forest, still a place to nurse himself while he howled for his loss.

Yes, I forgave him. I wasn't aware yet that a day could arrive when I might, inadvertently, become him. The connections between love, commemoration, and the passage of time are difficult to pinpoint. They crisscross and weave like game trails, and there is no one goal to be found at the end of any of them. But isn't that what poets are supposed to see when they look into darkness? A welcoming confusion? I didn't know, and I still don't. For me, all the shapes conform to the bright, empty space of someone who's leapt away, beyond my reach, a deer into the night.

71

The Book of Life After Death

LETTER TO CHRISTA MCAULIFFE, IN SPACE

Sarah Johnson

Christa McAuliffe was selected as the primary candidate for the NASA Teacher in Space Project on July 19, 1985. The STS 51-L crew died on January 28, 1986 when Challenger exploded after launch.
— NASA Biographical Data

In my room I think of you, beneath
    layers of blankets, between the heat
        of cotton sheets whose fibers scratch my knees;

I think of you years before I was born, years
    before I would know deep burning ache,
        the thrill and grief of giving more than my body

can offer, and then I'm in space,
    beyond oxygen—my chest constricts
        and when I breathe out I find you

looking up at my feet in stardust;
    your gaze holds each layer
        of sky, creates its own force

to stay—a suspension. You wait
    to gather more of yourself: pockets
        of gas, cobalt blues, amber sands.

To investigate your body I strain
    my limbs, draw taut my neck:
        a root compressed by soil, aching

to grow. My feet distend and then the rest
    of me swells, too, veins and legs,
        branches bloated with rain.

Essays & Poems

Then, the cold: my chest a capsule
    of blood, round cells that freeze,
        imperfect discs gathering weight

with breath. I become two parts, an opposition;
    is this what you meant when you looked
        into the camera, gathered your hands,

leaned into your pale blue suit and then
    slowly raised your chin? Could you
        have known the way my body would strain

each time I forced my eyes to catch in replay
    coils of smoke, all that would expand?
        I am only ever heat and dust.

WELCOMING THE LIGHT

Jesse Arthur Stone

I used to think mourning doves
were owls, as they hooted softly
in the distance, in the California dawn.
     This morning, as I woke up
in Aunt Verna's trailer, the first wave of sunlight
washed over it and the seams creaked
as though it, too, were awakening
after a long sleep.
     I came here to mourn
my departed aunt; to sell off
her possessions: piano, sheet music, even paintings
she made from photos I sent her
during my hitch in Europe. It has not been
easy: my aunt seen through her last days
and buried. And now my mother, who
came to help, lies in the hospital, a tube
down her throat.
     I go to visit her, and for the first time I see
tiny flutters of light in her eyes, looming
beneath thick glasses. Outside the window, a blimp
passes by, swollen and silent.
     Visiting over, I punch up Mom's pillow and kiss her
goodnight; take the elevator down
to the street and drive my aunt's old blue Caddy
back to her hushed mobile home.
     I make my bed on the floor, among
the half-boxed remnants of a life of music,
and welcome sleep like birds welcome the light
with their song.

MUJERES DIVINAS/DIVINE WOMEN

Sarah Chavera Edwards

The third of eight children in a Mexican mining town in Arizona, she endured the brunt of her mother's indifference and misplaced anger. A belt here, a chancla there, my grandmother's fire spirit was nearly extinguished at twelve. *"Era normal,"* she would say. What is normal about the subtle bruising down skinny girl arms? At sixteen, she knew her actual life existed elsewhere in a place she could not yet visualize. It laid beyond the lone river that flowed downhill from her family's farm. A rusted brown suitcase and a secret one-way ticket made the final decision a reality. Determined yet anxious, she took the 9 a.m. train to Winslow to begin her life's journey which would eventually lead to my grandfather and her home in Phoenix.

Decades would pass and her grandchildren would see beyond the gray hair and wrinkled hands to her inner identity that remained. The muted steadiness of her step and pure devotion in her eyes told us everything we needed to know. She would constantly ask if she could make us something to eat—a remnant of her own past Depression Era hunger. The soil of her ancestors rewarded all she touched with springs of life. The flower gardens decorating her ChaCha yellow house never dried despite the unrelenting summers. When her arms lovingly embraced me, it felt like both the first and the last time.

Despite her meager 6th grade education, she read constantly. She wrote page after page which would eventually become lost, leaving no testament to her inner thoughts. The gift of pen to paper was inherited through her blood. Several of us discovered this talent and explored both the heights and depths of its transcendence. A chance was gifted to us to take the oral Mexican storytelling tradition and give it a physical being.

When she succumbed to lung cancer, there was no comfort or understanding for her three youngest grandchildren, including me. Her casket was a soft glossy pink with gold trim and "The Yellow Rose of Texas" played as we sat in silent remembrance. Children and grandchildren spoke of her, telling tales of love while finding humor in sadness because that's how we cope with loss. I was not yet old enough to express myself that day because my poet voice was still in its infancy.

In eighteen years, I have only visited her grave once. She is buried with my grandfather in the city's veteran cemetery. It is a dusty place with rows and rows of plaques in the arid dirt. There is not a flower, tree, or even a patch of grass to be found. When I first saw it, I was disappointed that her final resting place was so drab and mediocre and unfitting. To me, this is not where she resides. Although her physical remains lay there, her spirit does not.

I call her name in front of my ofrenda every November and feel her draped over my shoulders like a quilt. The marigolds and La Virgen candles surround her pictures. I do not have any material thing of hers besides the last birthday gift she ever gave me. Knowing that I was a young bookworm she presented me a Barnes & Noble gift card with the words "I Love You" inscribed in her precise handwriting. That love has never faded and neither has the shape of her face in my memories.

She visits me in my dreams and we talk about the comings and go-ings of my life until, in the middle of our conversation, I realize she is long dead. Every time, I panic and ask her if she is okay. "Yes. You don't have to worry about me. I'm okay," she reassures me. We hold each other as I become aware that the hourglass sand is being spent and I will soon awake. When I finally do, I lay in the dark stillness and am thankful.

CHANNELING MOTHER

Charlene Stegman Moskal

I try to channel mother's essence,
tap into her strengths

even as I wonder
if she owned them

or did she, like me,
break down

f   r   a   g   i   l   e,
at the oddest moments,

like when her husband's ghost
rose translucent

in his favorite coffee cup?
Did the dam burst,

as she prepared and
ate his favorite food?

I see her reflection
in my mirror whose light

dances in broken shards
with unanswered questions.

THAW

Leah Claire Kaminski

I wake to thick shuffles
and thumps. Ice falling

uncages itself. How
can mere water

menace us so.
And what's to come

unburied. In Miami
I thought winter would be

entire. Now I know seasons
slip in and out. Belly of the arctic

sagging. Cache
of spring smuggled

back into winter. Picture of your
baby—your baby, mother—

with a full belly and thick
blond hair. Shadowed

and smiling in a cowboy costume
or nearly covered by tropical vine.

He was beautiful. No
wonder you didn't get rid

of one reminder of him,
totems moldering

Essays & Poems

with hurricane-damp.
Do you still look for him? After

the fire do you
still search at night

for sifting ghost-piles, precious ash?
Or what else do you find there?

ROSES IN HIS CHEEKS

Lisa del Rosso

I thought he was dead. I really did.

Out of the two of us, I always assumed I would go first, always. Yash only has things go wrong with him when he lifts too many big weights and then tears bits of his body that need to be repaired. Epilepsy can't be repaired and has no cure, so brain disorders trump athletic injuries. I win. I die first.

And that is what I was thinking, amongst other things, when Yash passed out in the chair, as I was trying to hold up his heavy body with one arm and a shoulder and staunch the blood with a cloth in the other hand. Neither was working. The gash on his forehead continued to flow and I had never thought about his weight before, but of course, muscle weighs more than fat, and so Yash was heavier than I thought he would be. He had also turned an alarming shade of wet sand: cold, skin clammy to the touch, underneath his eyes completely black, eyelids closed. This is what he'll look like dead, I thought, and he can't hear me and won't know me and will not respond to me. I wondered if all women who divorced men but continued to live with their former spouses still cared about them, dead or alive, but I did.

He had banged his head on that same, sharp metal corner of the bookshelf before, emitting the same cry each time, unusual for him, as he is an even-keel kind of person. The damage had always been minimal, barely a scratch, and never a suggestion by either one of us to change the position of his desk or perhaps not store the stepladder underneath the lowest shelf. Never occurred to us. Most accidents happen inside the home, we sometimes said to one another in mocking, parental tones, and then burst out laughing.

This time, I heard the cry and said, "Oh, what did you do now?"

Yash stood up, blood spewing from his head, a lump rising and not looking well at all. I made him sit down at the kitchen table, got him some juice, and he said, "I feel kind of woozy." And he went out, just like that. I was amazed that it happened so fast. One second he was there, one second gone, and suddenly that silt-gray color, with no re-

80

Essays & Poems

sponse to what I was saying. I sort of kept jostling him as best I could, holding him upright and with the same arm, I patted his back and continued talking to him.

"Yash, wake up, talk to me, you are not going to die on me today, no way, come on, wake up Yash, talk to me, no way are going to die on me today, wake up, wake up, wake up." And then I burst out laughing.

Stress does strange things to a person. Laughter. Why? Release? Disbelief at the situation I was in? Who knows? And while I was talking and laughing and rubbing Yash's back, I thought nine million things in those seconds or minutes he was out: about Natasha Richardson dying so young and vibrant over a fall she believed to be only silly, about being alone in the world without Yash in my life and that he needs to fight and come back from wherever he is now, just like I wanted him to do when we were married, fight for me, fight for us, but he didn't, couldn't, and why did I divorce him anyway and that's really mean payback, for Yash to die on me after I divorced him, really not fair at all and I have no chance of payback myself if he dies, I'm just left to suck it up for the rest of my life...

We are young, too young to be thinking about death, but since the epilepsy and even before that, I think about it more and more. I think a lot about quality rather than quantity, and because I have largely done what I wanted to do with my life, I'd be okay with it. Don't get me wrong: there will always be more stories to write and I would always elect the "more time" option if there was one, but I think that's the same for most people.

And then Yash woke up. Came to. Color back in his cheeks. "Hi," he said.

"Hi," I said.

Then I had a seizure. Now I know how I react to extreme stress. I had to rest on the floor, but didn't black out. I could talk through it, which was good because Yash was too weak to help me. He could only watch.

What a pair, I thought.

After we both composed ourselves, we went to the emergency room to make sure Yash did not have a concussion.

"I hope I don't get a needle," Yash said.

"I hope you do," I said, "because I thought you were dead."

81

"I'm sorry," he said.

"You should be," I said. And then I hugged him and never wanted to let him go.

He did not have a concussion. The doctor put some clear gel on his forehead, to close the gash. He did get a shot, for tetanus. I laughed only to myself. Yash told the doctor I had a seizure, which I brushed off, because there's nothing an ER can do for a seizure disorder other than admit me for tests, and I didn't want that.

We finally went home and considered filing down that edge of the bookshelf. We lay down on the still-made bed together, and I said to him, "I thought you were dead."

"I know," he said, "I'm sorry."

He closed his eyes, and I turned out the light. I kissed him and thought, I really hope I go first.

Essays & Poems

DEAD LETTER
Cathleen Calbert

Death's girlfriend is depressed because no one is sad anymore. People grieve but not longer than three weeks. Then they perform "personal rituals" for "closure" before they get back to "the business of living." They have people to do and things to see. Death's girlfriend doesn't want to see. She places cucumber slices on her eyelids and sinks into yet another tepid bath. Death can do nothing with her. She won't listen to reason. She won't mourn in moderation. She only lets him hold the soles of her wet feet as he swoons her into another afternoon. Finally, he pulls three envelopes from his vest pocket. It's against the rules, but what can he do? He's crazy about her. She opens the first letter. *Mock apple pie,* she reads, *will never taste like the real thing.* She rips into the second. *Please pick up my dry cleaning.* Slowly, she unfolds the third. *Dear Daughter,* she reads but can't go on: the words swim away from her. Death looks at the single sheet. "Ah," he says. "An idiolect I don't know."

83

THE LOFT

Will Stenberg

for R

In that dim loft we performed
the original mysteries.

My confusions circled like crows and cawed.

Each the other's captive,
overheated kids in mutual kidnap.

The purity of these early initiations:
the naked faces,
the inelegant fumbles.

She had the biggest eyes,
and a short life ahead of her,
and the biggest eyes.

Forever her softness abides,
forever her beloved form,
forever that dark loft

where death was not permitted, where the work of love began.

CALAVERITA A MI VIEJA VERSIÓN

Dulce Solís

¿Se podrá hacer la calaverita a la versión
que una fue perdiendo con los años?
Soy otra, ahora que me convertí en madre,
ya no me va a encontrar la flaca.
Pues a la que buscaba
ya la han cambiado los desengaños.
Lo que antes me importaba e intrigaba
 ahora ya ni destaca.

¿Me puedo poner metalingüística
en mi poema?
Hablar de la que era antes
de que fuera a terapia.
Cuando todo frente a mí
me representaba un problema.
Mi vida era revuelta, caótica, sin sentido
y fragmentaria.

A esa ya te la puedes llevar Catrina,
la que era antes de la llegada de mi hijo.
Esa temerosa, ansiosa
y que a la vida no le veía sentido.
A la que no importaba lo que hiciera,
en nada encontraba regocijo.
Y la que estaba siempre en su cabeza
el futuro incierto o el pasado perdido.

Quizá el siguiente año Calaca
vuelvas por la otra adaptación.
Porque es un proceso que no termina,
la muerte de quienes pensábamos que éramos.

The Book of Life After Death

Se vuelve un ciclo
que da vida a la nueva percepción.
Y hace que nos volvamos quienes somos
y empecemos a ser quienes quisiéramos.

Essays & Poems

HERE & NOW

Letisia Cruz

We were home. It was a Monday—my 46th birthday. The sun was a giant orange balloon playing hide-and-seek behind the slash pines that morning. Bigwig and I watched a bobcat waltz along the canal. We scurried from one sliding glass door to the other, watching her strut behind the chain link fence.

The lanai we had dreamed of for years was installed in a matter of hours that week. On Thursday we ventured out to the screen enclosure. Bigwig's legs twitched with excitement. We inhaled wet moss and scanned the perimeter for lizards and limpkins. No bobcats that day. I was grateful to have that space to share with him. A space where we could safely watch ospreys swoop in for lunch and alligators drift by. That afternoon we watched a pair of wild rabbits hop along the perimeter and a parade of squirrels dash along the fence.

Three days later, Bigwig was gone.

In some stories, the loss of a pet comes first. The child rushes home from school only to find their beloved cat is gone. All the hard questions that follow are answered neatly, with the reassurance of heaven and life after death. Some of us accept these answers as gospel. Life moves through us, and we learn to live with loss. We more or less leave childhood and believe ourselves grown, fully formed humans who are somehow better prepared to encounter death. Then it comes again. We lose a parent or a sibling or a partner, and we realize we were never prepared.

In other stories, it happens in reverse. There is no cat. Death swoops in like an osprey and takes the parent first.

It was a cold day in December—always December. We had been to the eye doctor that morning. Two weeks after my ninth birthday. My pupils were dilated on the drive home. Cold hugged the car seats and clung to the windows. My father parked the car and we ran inside. Fog filled the hall. Death is quiet, even when it isn't. In our logical mind, we know it is bound to come for us one day. But one day is far from here. Far from now.

87

The Book of Life After Death

My father walked into the hallway. Two gunshots pierced the air and time fractured. A flood of blood and sirens wailed. That was the last time I saw him.

What we do in this life is busy ourselves with the things we want to expect—we cook and we eat. We clean the house and we go for a walk. We sleep and we work. We try our best, always try our best. We convince ourselves that if we do these things life may one day be kind to us. Because we have been so good. Because we have tried so hard.

In my own story, all the neat answers never fit. I never accepted the gospel. The questions remained, growing within me, becoming my own religion. I imagined, as everyone does, that I was somehow better prepared this way. Somehow more resilient.

When I was 15, I watched my mother's skull get pummeled by my stepfather's fists. Sunday boxing, we called it. Ordinary. For years, we tip-toed around the attic trying to become invisible. Eventually, we did what all black and blue birds do—we migrated south and learned to survive. The first sunrise I remember watching was on 72nd avenue in Miami Beach. I was 27. The sun's rays stretched across the Atlantic. I sat motionless on the sand waiting for those arms to reach me. Waiting. While I waited, the planets continued to orbit around the same sun, and every day I woke up a tiny bit older. Tiny.

Almost unrecognizably so.

Almost.

But the difference between living and surviving is vast. It's ironic, given the amount of time we spend screaming—outright howling into the abyss—how badly we want to survive quietly. To be overlooked. One minute we're here talking talking talking. The next we're permanently silent. Death will not overlook us. No matter how quiet we are. No matter how hard we try. This is the one thing we know for certain. It's the same thing we spend our lives trying to forget.

As a child, I often wondered how the kind of disappearance that happens when we die is possible. How is it that we can be here one instant—a living, breathing being—and gone the next? Where does the part that is intrinsically us go? All of the questions remained until they were almost comfortable. I remember running around the cemetery where my father was newly buried admiring the tombstones. Being nine years old—time was foreign to me. My entire existence

Essays & Poems

was a quick sprint. I had no concept of permanence, of the persistence of emptiness.

When I was 39, Bigwig walked into our apartment on Normandy Isle. He was a tiny kitten with big bunny ears. I loved him instantly, differently, in a way I had never loved anyone. Bigwig filled entire gratitude journals. He made everything that had come before necessary—all of the pieces forgiven. He was magic. I wanted to hug him forever, to squish his fluffy paws and watch him nap in the sun, to protect him from everything. To be with him always.

Six and half years later on a Sunday in December he was gone. It was wrong—he was too young. But that's life, isn't it? Extraordinary and beautiful one second. Moss flowing toward the sun. A symphony of birds. An orange balloon playing hide-and-seek in the sky. Dizzying. Dazzling.

Then gone.

When Bigwig died the sun burst instantly. All the light was gone. I had journeyed along dark roads. I had allowed myself to believe that I was more resilient for it, but the opposite was true. That unflinching black hole we call loss consumed me. I clung to all of our birds even as they became memory. My here and now was no longer. And I asked myself why? Why did losing Bigwig bring me back to same dark hall where my father was killed?

If our purpose on this earth is to grow in our capacity to love, animals are our greatest teacher. They bring us back to our childhood selves—to a time when we knew how to love unconditionally. They are our constant companions—always there to greet us, even if disapprovingly so, when we come home. Through them we become truer versions of ourselves. We learn to have hope, to believe in everything, to open our arms and give love infinitely.

This is how we are made to remember. Loss marks us in ways we are never prepared for. Love is the ocean spilling on the shore. Again and again. Here and now and never after. Storms pass through us. We endure our own apocalypses. And if we are lucky, we were home once.

The Book of Life After Death

EVEN HEAVEN REQUIRES YOUR SURVIVAL

Susan L. Leary

There are flowers inside other flowers
     & there are drugs inside the flowerpots.

Shame laced inside snowfall & tar. Brother,
     I'm afraid to say you walked out on your life

trying to make a home of it. What fortune, then, to be
     met by the hailing of a new sun & the lesser light

of its aftermath. Even in paradise, there is an aftermath
     & this time, you are to be a better host. How to say it

plainly? What happened to you as a child was not all that
     interesting. Brother, only in a world that takes you hostage,

                     are you free.

Essays & Poems

MARINER

Emilee Wirshing

My grandfather knew the stars
and now he is among them,
an unnamed comet that is
not a lifeboat, but not unlike
a vessel that could take one
to safety, his coordinates are
unclear but I will look up
and know him in the glimmer
of something vast and outlasting.
He and I have peeled the cosmos
like an orange, measured
the murkiness in constellations
and myths, the navigator
need not question the contents
of the sky, the inventory of antiquity,
neither he nor I ask for proof
of the luminaries, just how to track
our way back when we are lost
at sea. Some of his stories
are fantasies, others are maps
measured in white caps
that lap at the edge of the night.

The Book of Life After Death

DELUGE

James Joseph Brown

World, we sit beside
your seven seas

hasten ourselves until
newsworthy and steadfast

the fish cry at night
when they bubble and dream

once I thought I was flying
but really, I was a fish

so high above the ocean
floor the coral mourned me

into the sky
we rose with the rivers

deleted the shores
built broadside galleries

to petition the dead
for darkness and rain.

Essays & Poems

QUESTIONS ON DEATH

Shane Mason

What sounds can be heard after death?
And how loud is the volume?
Can I hear the lyrics and melody,
a new Rihanna song released after I'm dead?

What happens to one's visions?
Surely there is some spiritual cloud database to store these, right?
Can I still see my memories, my wedding day?

When someone touches a cold body, can the cold body feel them
back?
Do they feel the warmth of the live person like a blanket? Or maybe
it will feel like fire?
Can I still feel the pleasure of a pedicure massage?

Medical journals refer to organ deaths as though each body part is
an independent being.
Yet none of them are actually independent.
So how do you live when one of them dies?

Does one's blood dry up and crust, hardening the veins?
Or does it continue in liquid form, no longer able to flow, stagnant as
a swamp?
Can I still bleed?

The Book of Life After Death

ONCE UPON A DREAM DRESS
Kelly Jean Fitzsimmons

The Obituary

Helen Anne Lind
February 8, 1943 - August 22, 2019

Gloucester, MA—Helen Anne Lind was born in Maine on February 8, 1943. She grew up in Melrose, Mass., attending the Gooch and Roosevelt elementary schools and graduated in 1961 from Melrose HS where she enjoyed dancing and acting, performing in a school production of Carousel. She later attended the Museum School in Boston where she won an award for design and fabrication of a jewelry art piece. She worked in the Display and Graphics Department at Filene's in Boston while living on Broad Street there. This gave her access to Boston nightlife, where she gained an appreciation for modern jazz and music in general.

Her love of music and art brought her to Gloucester, which she considered home, always returning there no matter where else life took her. She started a very successful graphic arts business, and, in fact, Helen Anne is responsible for many of the recognizable logos in and around Cape Ann, including the Cape Ann Chamber of Commerce, CATA, and the Cape Ann Vernal Pond Team, that are still in use today.

She also unknowingly shared a special connection with Kelly Jean Fitzsimmons, the niece of Angela Ciaramitaro, a lifelong resident of Gloucester who was her calligraphy student and friend. Helen Anne never met Angela's niece but years ago, when she was living in a summer rental on Eastern Point, the artist had the habit of going through the garbage of her affluent neighbors in search of material for her work.

Once, Helen Anne discovered four trash bags filled with formal gowns and threw a big party where her women friends, Angela included, drank wine, tried on the gowns, and chose a dress to take home.

Kelly Jean's family moved away from Cape Ann when she was five years old. While she, too, always returns no matter where else life

94

Essays & Poems

takes her, Gloucester has never felt like home. As a child, she spent many a lonely summer day hiding in the upstairs closet of her aunt's house on Liberty Street after getting in trouble for acting out. The young overweight girl spent hours staring up at the creamy, off-white vintage dress with a plunging neckline accentuated by a beaded waist that flared into a flowing skirt—one that would flirtatiously billow up over a heating vent—and imagined Angela wearing the dress to a costume party as Marilyn Monroe. Growing up, Kelly Jean fantasized about the day when her boobs would be big enough and, more importantly, her waist small enough to wear the dream dress to prom.

The Origin Story

Once upon a time, an unworn dress languished inside the impenetrable pitch of the wardrobe. The yellow slant of light, accompanied by the rustling of fabric and welcoming creak of the door, no longer excited. Long ago, the illumination of the wardrobe's bleak void signaled possibility, the chance to be chosen. Then as days piled into months, raising a tower of dark years that imprisoned the dress and her sisters inside, the opening no longer held the promise of an elegant evening out.

Now fear flooded in with the light as the wardrobe door didn't creak but cracked wide to reveal the calculating peer of the Mistress's pinched glare. Clawed hands, adorned with oversized rings—the weight of the opulent stones spinning the metal loops around twiggy fingers, boney knuckles blocking their escape—pawed and pushed the dress and her sisters from side to side. The long nails of the Mistress, each tipped with a perfect streak of white, tickled over bits of lace and smoothed back wrinkles while flared nostrils investigated the musk of forgotten fabric. Anxiety rustled through the locked-away dresses: Who of us will remain when the lady completes her cleanse?

The dress had never been worn. Once, she'd been taken out in what was the most thrilling moment of the young frock's life. The Mistress held up the silken ivory, flattening the fine detail of the beaded bodice across the thirsty thump of her human heart. Holding one side of the flared skirt aloft, she frowned at the sight of the long willows of her legs jutting out, their shade of pale sallow in comparison. The unworn

The Book of Life After Death

dress saw her fate framed in the standing mirror. Crow's feet marched along the edges of the Mistress's narrowed eyes, the freckled leather of her sunken décolletage flushing hot red as she stared at their shared reflection with royal disparagement. My time is up. The dress was certain she would soon disappear like so many sisters who'd come and gone. Nevertheless, that day the Mistress granted the Marilyn-Esque dress a reprieve, placing her back inside the holding pattern of the wardrobe. To wait.

Many of her sister dresses had been chosen, returning from grand adventures with flowery perfume clinging to their fabric or smugly flaunting their new, crisp smell of chemical cleanliness. Those dresses whispered to each other in the dark about art auctions, majestic ballrooms, and the incessant fear of cocktail sauce. The unworn dress could do nothing but wait for the day when she might be part of the story.

Then came the reckoning. The wardrobe flung open, its heavy oak door landing with a thunk against the slender brass lamp that stood guard. The lamp sent forth a palpable shudder of warning, having borne witness to the Mistress deep in the throes of a whirlwind purge. That day, there was no careful sliding of padded hangers back and forth across the hanging bar as the Mistress performed careful deliberations. Instead, she yanked and tossed, snatched and grabbed, blue tributaries snaking their way across her palms pulsing from frenzy. The unworn dress was ripped away from her hanger and shoved alongside her sisters into the gaping mouth of a large, rubbery black bag.

The fierce expediency of the wardrobe's mass expulsion left the tossed-away dress fighting to catch her breath. Once caught, the stench of stretched rubber made her want to retch, but she was packed too tightly alongside her sisters to do so. The press of pearls dug into her back, and the flirty wisp of faux fur brushing at her hemline did little to distract from the balled-up darkness. With a swish and swoosh underscored by much jostling, the bag journeyed forth. At last, the unworn dress was finally being taken out. But far from the manner of her choosing. The sail was short, the landing hard, and the softness she and her sisters provided each other did little to cushion the harsh reality of the concrete curb they'd been set upon. Their sudden exodus

96

ending in another holding pattern. This one a click of a metronome compared to the full symphony of time inside the wardrobe. Still, uncertainty stretched the span the unworn dress spent as roadside trash into infinity. Moments or eons, perhaps, slipped by in the smother of darkness before the bag's mouth yawned open to reveal two suns — one, a woman's face shining as round and bright as the fiery orb of the second sun hovering behind her shoulder.

The soft apples of the stranger's cheeks flushed a joyful red, excitemnt murmuring through the feathered tendrils of her hair. The salt and pepper strands licked free from the paisley scarf tied around her head. The edges of her fingers tinged with ink; paint splattered across the back of an elbow. Despite her disheveled appearance, the woman's manner was as precise as the thin rectangular glasses positioned atop the smooth slope of her nose. Her curious fingers wove their way into the bag with a careful reverence the dress had long forgotten. This woman didn't scrutinize the unworn dress and her sisters for their flaws or treat them like lumps of cloth and buttons. Her unadorned lips pinked with pleasure as she surveyed her found treasure. She breathed in the velvety musk of memories hidden at the heart of each dress mixed with her own recollection of nights filled with dancing, music, and laughter. The woman beheld the tossed-away frocks with the eyes of an artist who looks at the world and sees what's yet to be created. She didn't see trash but the promise of *Once upon a time...* yet to be told.

It would have been easy for the Artist to yank up the bags and dump the dresses into the trunk of her car in the same unceremonious manner as they'd been ejected from the wardrobe. Instead, the unworn dress felt her every silken fiber flood with love when the Artist pulled each abandoned dress forth, straightening and folding them over her arm, one by one.

The dress embraced her sisters as they hugged themselves into the arms of the Artist, a return to dignity. The blaze of their shared joy rivaled the summer sun of this brave new world.

Then came the bacchanal. The unworn dress and her sisters did not have their shoulders slipped around the stiff corners of hangers but found themselves strewn across the couch, chairs, and plush rug of the sage-smudged room. Joviality replaced the fear tingling their stitches as the Artist strategically draped each dress. Her past life in the wardrobe slipped into oblivion as an unheard sound rang through the air, the silver bells of feminine laughter. The room filled with freckled hands, wiggling toes, warm breasts, fresh-smelling necks, and pungent armpits. The dresses flew about, passed, caressed, and held up in front of one potential new wearer to the next. Is this what dancing feels like? The unworn dress wondered, spinning from the uncut high of light and life outside the wardrobe. Landing against the soft swell of a hip, the dress delighted in the patter of the woman's heart, which quickened as her soon-to-be Mistress admired herself draped in the saucy flare of the silken skirt. Chosen! Taken home by the soft-hipped woman, the dress imagined future evenings out, wondering if it was possible for them to be even more magical than tonight. Brilliant adventures tip-toed along the horizon line of her imagination as she was freshened by chemical cleanliness and slipped inside a clear plastic sheath. The unworn dress then found herself stored away inside another square of darkness.

No longer hanging alongside her sisters but packed into an overstuffed closet. Her new neighbors were a wool peacoat, which reeked of fish and forgotten smoke, and thick sweaters, their knit nubby and attitudes aloof. The creamy dress wondered if they resented her stature, hanging high on the back of the splintered door. Her broken heart knew, however, that she was no better than any other article of used clothing that lived within. The long anticipation of her happy ending yielded nothing but another infinity of waiting. Alone in the dark.

Years chewed away at decades and, occasionally, the dress was considered. But never taken out. Never worn. Tired of waiting, the unworn dress fell into a dreamless sleep inside the coffin of her dry-cleaning bag.

One morning, a sunny slant warmed her fabric as the dress awoke to an unfamiliar touch. A small finger crept inside the clear plastic to give her skirt a tender caress, tracing a tiny, chewed nail up along the embroidered bodice. The door pulled wide; salted air punctuated by the distant caw of gulls cut through the stale gloom of the closet. A young girl, face as cherubic as the rounded swell of her tummy, peered up at the dress with red, puffy eyes. Her chest hitched from the fading tremors of an epic tantrum.

Essays & Poems

The lonely girl stared up at the unworn dress, the dimple in her chubby cheek imploding into an avalanche of awe brought forth by the blossom of her smile. The dress returned the Girl's gaze, seeing nothing in her but promise. The pair fell in love at first sight. A love that meant no more waiting, no more darkness, no more tears. Together came with the certainty that one day the Girl would grow into a woman, slip on the dress, and they would be the story.

The Fairy Tale

The magic of the night when the dress could no longer call herself unworn exceeded all expectations. The ballroom felt more cavernous than majestic — and reeked of a pungent aroma that reminded the dress of the old shoes lurking in the back of the wardrobe — but its youthful inhabitants crackled like live wires. Gowns caught the eye as they twirled through the darkness, some long and formal, similar to her lost sisters, others sucked up every shimmer of light with their fierce sequins. Each dress, however, gave their miniature Mistresses the aura of a Goddess.

The goers of this ball were peculiar in that, similar to the Girl, they were children adorned in the costume of adulthood standing on the precipice of futures yet untold. The finely dressed children clustered, the air around them buzzing from the anticipation of the announcement the pale-faced Adult stood before the microphone to make. The Girl, the Princess, whose warm fingers kept caressing the dress as she slipped the gown over her shoulders and slid the metal zipper up her side, watched the spectacle devoid of emotion. The Princess didn't share the excitement of the crowd around her, believing her unremarkable future to be set in stone. When they called out her name, the Princess didn't react to the rippling murmurs that erupted into cheers of Congratulations! The dress, however, could feel the emotion quaking the young woman's limbs from within, heart threatening to burst through the silken folds cupping the budding swell of her breasts.

The dress and her Princess stepped into a pool of adoration. The dress trembled with the knowledge of how a moment in the light can be enough to sustain years of solitude. All eyes watched as the glittering tiara, adorned with an S-shaped swoop of sparkling stones at the

99

The Book of Life After Death

center of its delicate band, was placed onto the Princess's head, transforming her into the Queen.

The Epilogue

Kelly Jean spun so many stories about the dream dress as a child. When Helen Anne passed away, she learned the true tale was far more fantastic than any she'd imagined.

"You have a connection to Helen, you know," Angela said when Kelly Jean mentioned that someone shared Helen Anne's obituary on Facebook, and she'd recognized the name of her aunt's friend.

That's when Angela told her niece the origin story of her prom dress.

"Do you still have the dress?" Kelly Jean asked, comforted by the thought of the dream dress still being there, hanging in the closet on Liberty Street. Her connection to Helen Anne, to Angela, to Gloucester.

"Yes, you know me, I never throw anything away," her aunt laughed. After they hung up, Kelly Jean read the obituary again, struck anew by the last line:

Of course Helen Anne would love people to remember her with a smile and a bit of style.

The paragraphs in italics are from Helen Anne Lind's obituary as published in the *Gloucester Times* on October 29, 2019.

Essays & Poems

REPRIEVE
Linda Michel Cassidy

The storm let up long enough for Lorraine to bury her husband. The service was held at a tucked-away neighborhood cemetario, down a dirt road, ruts gouged and frozen. The graves are marked with local surnames, several lives notably short.

An off-duty mariachi played guitar in the classical style, singing the Ave Maria in Latin. The men in pressed jeans, polished boots, black cowboy hats; the women in long skirts, pants beneath, hair tied back against the raging wind.

This time of the year, the early edges of winter: the plastic flowers attached to the wrought iron hairpin gates with twist ties. Weathered toys, framed photos, American flags, love letters in sandwich bags, the occasional bottle.

With a propane torch, you warm the ground enough to dig in a pick, then move on to a shovel. The squall whips the water out of your eyes, leaves a streak of dried salt on your cheek. The hail comes right after you toss the dirt.

BUFFER

DeAnna Beachley

I dropped everything—drove
the four hours to be with you and your dad
after your mother passed.

Remembered how she and I
talked about history books, swapped recipes,
kept her occupied.

You and I stayed in her room
the night after she died. She appeared to me,

sometime in the late hours.
I stirred, walked into the en suite

saw her in the mirror
slightly fuzzy and not whole—a hologram.

She stayed with me as I walked
through the frosty room back to bed—

told me of her great love
the man who promised to take her away
gave her the little tin box
after he enlisted
Where's my anchor inscribed on the lid
St. Paul, Minn. scratched onto the surface
with a penknife

the man who died in battle
the life she envisioned with him—gone
in an instant.

Essays & Poems

Your father came along months after this,
a rebound, a compromise, a companion,
but not equal.

I asked her, *why come to me? Why not
your daughter?*

She's not ready.

I was the buffer—there for you,
and now, this one last service
I could provide.

THE CRADLE

Celia Lisset Alvarez

My husband got rid of the cradle
while I was away with a friend.
Tidied up, changed the bed.
It took me a minute to register
the empty space where my babies
used to be.

I demanded to know where it went,
envisioning a garbage pile
full of flies. *It's in the shed,*
he said, and I ran to find it,
propped it up, lay down clean,
fresh sheets. And looked at it.

My babies are four and three.
There'll be no more babies for me.
I had meant to clean it up,
donate it, have it live on in
some other family. I couldn't
bring myself to wipe away the grit
of the little hands that had circled it,
so eager to get out, practicing to walk.

I folded the bedclothes
into the drawer. Then I collapsed
the four posts of the crib,
like a morning flower folding
in on itself at sunset. I put it
in its carrying case. I took it

Essays & Poems

back to the shed, leaned it
against the toys and tricycles,
the dolls without a head.
The clutter of my life,
useless as the dead. One day,
I thought, I'll be ready to clear
out this place. For now, however,
I turned around and went to bed.

ROPA VIEJA Y ROM THE SPACEKNIGHT: EN LA CASA DE ABUELA

Jarret Keene

"Oye, abuelita," I said, bringing to the sink my finished plate. There was nothing to scoop into the trash because I'd nearly licked the ceramic clean. "Dominoes."

"Pues. What about Go Fish?" She sat at the kitchen table in her house dress and slippers, sucking her teeth and changing the station on the transistor radio she kept by the sink. Static. R&B. Car commercial. Finally she landed on something she could tolerate: Air Supply's "All Out of Love," its tinny melody filling the room.

"Okay. I wash, you dry."

"Just put them in the rack, sweetie."

"Sí, por supuesto." I warmed the water and squirted a bunch of electric-blue Dawn liquid into the filling basin.

"Not too much."

"I know, abuela." Suds began rising and, eager to complete the task quickly, I placed a sponge under the faucet.

"Déjalo. Slow down."

"Yes, abuela."

"We have an hour before *That's Incredible.*"

"There's a martial-arts expert tonight. He's using *nunchaku* to knock an apple from a woman's head."

"Is it dangerous?"

"I hope so."

"We have time," she said, "to play Go Fish and Dominoes. I don't want to see *el fin del mundo.*" She didn't like watching the news, full of violence and perversion. She said Dan Rather was a *cabrón y cagado.* News personalities sickened her. The nightly news bored me, unless the ABC/NBC/CBS talking head did a segment on the disturbing popularity of the band KISS among young audiences or the unlikely success of *Dance Fever* — my favorite show after having seen pop-rocker Rick Springfield perform his hit "I've Done Everything for You" and then serve as a judge, scoring the couples who competed on the show.

106

Essays & Poems

In the year 1981, I didn't care about the shooting of President Reagan or of Pope John Paul II. I didn't care about the striking air-traffic controllers or the space shuttle (it looked to me like a tubby school-bus version of *Battlestar Galactica*'s Viper Mark One fighter) or the foofy wedding of Prince Charles and Princess Diana. What I cared about was, well, the apocalyptic, face-melting power of the tablet fragments in *Raiders of the Lost Ark*. What I delighted to ponder was the engineering savvy that went into the DeLorean's gull-wing doors. What I yearned for was to ogle the star-spangled hot pants of Wonder Woman, with her long jet-black hair and skin-tight, golden-palmed top that accentuated her boobs. Whatever was covered by local and national news was for grown-ups whose imaginations had died; now they were content to comprehend the brain-deadening chaos of reality with the help of teleprompter-reading men with sculpted hair. I wanted newscasters to be like pro wrestler Ric Flair, brash and garish and physical and, well, muscular.

Which is why, when my mother took me to the pillbox library around the corner from my house, I had checked out *Arnold: The Education of a Bodybuilder*. I read not a word of the book — it wasn't a comic teeming with little speech balloons, after all — and gazed at the photos of the three-time Mr. Universe for inspiration. Pages splayed on the floor beside me, I struggled to complete a push-up, dipping my face to the carpet in a wretched simulation of a feat of strength.

"*Cuerpo recto,*" she'd scold, with the same voice she used to point out the parts of her car that I'd washed poorly or not at all, one of only a handful of chores that she ever assigned me.

I groaned dramatically, trying to communicate with my strained visage how Herculean a simple push-up was.

"If you do those *cada día,*" she said, "your muscles will grow *como* Lou Ferrigno."

"*Sí, abuela! Como* Arnold!"

"I have *ropa vieja* ready for you when you're done. *Corre!*"

"Ah!" I yelped, my thin arms trembling and burning from exertion.

Herbie Mann's disco-flute instrumental "Superman" was appropriately (or ironically) playing on the radio, and she cranked up the volume and danced — which for her consisted of robotically swiveling her blue mumu-draped body left and right, like C-3PO floundering to recall something important. It made me laugh, and I collapsed in a mirth spasm. I'm still laughing.

Hey, God, it's 2022, and I want a time machine.

I lived *con mi abuelita* for the first 18 years of my life. In her nourishing presence, I absorbed U.S. postwar popular culture sitting cross-legged in front of her color Zenith, which displayed everything from Harmony Gold's TV-anime series *Robotech* to country-music variety show *Hee Haw*. I stewed in commercial entertainment by merely sitting at her kitchen table, where we played the Mattel card game *UNO*. In between endless rounds, she would dollop me helping after helping of Bill Cosby-branded chocolate Jell-O pudding with the radio blasting Hall and Oates's "Kiss on My List." In effect, she cocooned me in her sturdy home constructed of concrete blocks, situated along what was then a depressing stretch of West Dr. Martin Luther King Jr. Boulevard, four potholed lanes that intersected with brackish, manatee-inhabited Hillsborough River, a short walk from then-Tampa Stadium.

We lived in a low-income area teeming with fried-chicken joints, malt-liquor billboards, and immigration services. Nearby parks were humid swelters of bloodthirsty mosquitoes. I had a banged-up Huffy bicycle like all *los blancos pobres* in the neighborhood, towheaded shit-kickers who pummeled me at school for being a Dungeons & Dragons-playing gifted student—in other words, a nerd. But abuela didn't want me running with them and getting in trouble or beaten up. She usually urged me to stay with her and watch an episode of *Lawrence Welk Show* or *The Fall Guy*. More often than not I accepted her invitation, because how could I resist such visual treats? The former offered the Semonski Sisters, a sextet of gorgeous blonde Polish-Irish girls who sang like angels and made my chest tighten; the latter chronicled the semi-comic misadventures of a Hollywood stuntman who bounty-hunted thugs for extra cash between movie productions.

No matter what I sat down to watch with her, abuela offered me a snack. The world outside was harsh, ragged, but *en la casa de abuela* life was sugary sweet and artificially colorful. There was so much to observe, so much to learn about life beyond the dirty streets of downtown Tampa—and so much to chow as I savored the images, characters, stories. Even today, in my most anxious moments, I dream of

Essays & Poems

returning to her house. I dream of sitting at her kitchen table with the two-issue (*The Uncanny X-Men* #141-142) "Days of Future Past" storyline before me, turning each colorful page as I sip the juice she has squeezed for me using oranges from the tree in her front yard, a fresh drink full of pulp and flavor. My abuela putters in the kitchen, scrubbing a burner on the stove. My abuela goes outside for a spell, pinning laundry to the line in the yard outside the window. My abuela comes back inside to feed me a snack of guava and crackers. She pours me a big cold glass of chocolate milk.

My parents lived in the adjacent, cramped, code-violating, three-bedroom addition. Their puny Quasar was black-and-white. The meals my father prepared for us were extreme: either vitamin-rich and cruciferous or pure wartime-poverty fare. On some nights, my father prepared steamed broccoli and grilled whitefish; on others he served up SOS — shit on a shingle — ground beef and cream of mushroom soup on wheat toast. He was a tremendous firehouse cook, though, and could dish Cuban food better than anyone alive, but he didn't spoil me like his mother-in-law did. No, he honestly believed Fig Newtons counted as cookies, when any child will tell you: *Hell no, they don't.* I was always ravenous, so I devoured my father's meals with gusto, mopped my plate, picked the fishbone slivers from my teeth, and scarfed my nightly allotment of four Newtons. I loved my father, but when he put on his uniform and left in the early morning to work his 24-hour shift at the firehouse before I dressed for school, I could already taste my abuela's dinnertime meal of crispy fried plantains, hearty *ropa vieja*, and garlic-drenched yuca. Or her Cuban picadillo with canned carrots in butter. *Arroz y frijoles negros* with a cob of sweet corn. *Arroz amarillo con pollo* — bright yellow, mouth-watering. On the nights my father worked, my mother, my sister, and I would sit at my abuela's table and eat the food she prepared, then play cards or dominoes together. Around 7 o'clock we'd all watch something like the *Muppet Show* before it was time for my younger sister to prepare for bed back at our house. I was allowed to stay with abuela and sleep over on her couch as long as I turned in before 9 o'clock.

I never tucked in that early, because abuela let me stay up late with her and watch absolutely everything, including Johnny Carson and *Saturday Night Live*. By midnight, my brain was fatigued from over-

The Book of Life After Death

stimulation. Finally, I'd drift asleep, dreaming of KITT, a weapons-festooned and intelligent black Pontiac Firebird that supported David Hasselhoff's crimefighting character on *Knight Rider*. The next morning at my elementary school, bleary-eyed, I would pencil-render pictures on wide-ruled paper, elaborate tableaus of violence such as: KITT, "Mean" Joe Greene, and Daisy Duke fighting the chrome-armored Cylons of *Battlestar Galactica* as bass guitar-wielding Gene Simmons of KISS, comedian Steve Martin with his *pluck-plonking* banjo, and baton-swinging Welk and his orchestra (their instruments replaced with machine guns)—a conflict of epic pop-culture icons taking the place on the desert terrain of Planet Tatooine.

Abuela loved TV shows about automotive and aerial technology. She and I together watched *A-Team*, *CHiPs*, *Airwolf*, *Miami Vice*, and *Blue Thunder*. She loved watching villains receive their comeuppance from tech-enhanced law enforcement. She especially enjoyed, in the late '80s, *Cops*, a dismal ride-along-with-the-police docuseries. She would sing the "Bad Boys" theme to me when she learned I'd done something wrong—get in a fight, bomb a test—at my high school. Abuela loved professional wrestling, especially *Championship Wrestling from Florida*, featuring the shit-talking spectacle of Dusty Rhodes and Ric Flair, and the towering menace of Andre the Giant. She loved *telenovelas*, which I watched with her in an effort to speak better Spanish and to study beautiful Mexican actresses who seemed, in every scene, to wear swimsuits at the beach and negligees in their lavish, white-columned homes.

Abuela was patient with me, encouraging my childhood efforts to imitate and perform the pop entertainment that sustained me throughout the 1970s and 1980s. After studying Michael Jackson's moonwalk on TV, I attempted to sock-slide backward like my musical hero in the tiled area by the front door, placing one foot in front of the other, and the other with my toes pressed to the tile. Then I slid my heel of the first foot along and into the floor while snapping both feet as they swapped positions. Repeat, and there I was, doing it. I was moonwalking!

"*Bueno*," she said. "Go!"

"But Abuela, there's only so much tile here," I whined.

"In a circle! *Círculo!*"

110

Essays & Poems

Duh. I just needed to moonwalk in a circle to keep from running out of smooth tile. MJ had done the same thing himself in the clip I had seen on TV. I was shaky at first, but after a few tries I had it down cold, gliding and wheeling, faster and faster.

"*Rápido*," she said, getting up from her comfy chair with a sigh. "You want rice pudding while I'm up?"

"*Si, abuela*," I said, spinning like a lunar fiend. "With extra cinnamon!"

"Okay. Don't forget your push-ups!"

Sweet memories of being spoiled rotten.

Abuela supported me in my first literary scratches and scribblings. I drew comics about my dog Willy and my cat Leo. Endowed with superpowers from having eaten radioactive dog food mistakenly shipped to the U.S. from Hiroshima, my family pets fought crime in local settings—thwarting robbery at the credit union where my father deposited his paychecks and rescuing hard-partying teenagers who had crashed their boat into a dock along the nearby Hillsborough River. After I completed the layouts, pencils, and speech bubbles for my three- to four-page stories, I'd show them to Abuela. She studied each smudged 8x11, no doubt feigning to appreciate and comprehend the hapless blizzard of bizarre action sequences I'd rendered, even taking time to read the fake ads I'd included for make-believe products like "an officially licensed Smurfs soda pop, manufactured by Shasta in California."

"What does it taste like?" she asked.

I shrugged. "Maybe like grape, since they don't make blueberry."

Abuela nodded; she enjoyed sipping a Shasta now and then, and she was always buying me multiple six-packs of Shasta beverages from Kash n' Karry, a Florida-based chain of grocery stores. Shasta was cheap and offered a broader range of flavors than the Coke and Pepsi brands.

Abuela had spent the first five years of her life in New York City in desperate poverty, then moved to Tampa when her father found a job at a corrugation plant by the port. For a while, her family did better, but then her father died of typhus when she was just 10 years old. She saw him displayed in his coffin during the funeral and dreamed of-

111

The Book of Life After Death

ten—for the remaining seventy years of her life—of him popping out of the ground to speak with her about her life and her children, and me. He explains her future—*my* future—for her in these eerie dreams.

"What does he say about me?" I asked her once.

"That you will be a great artist."

"*Por qué?*" I say.

"Why does he say this or how does he know?"

"*Como sabe eso?*"

"The dead know the future."

"What kind of artist will I be?"

"A writer. Definitely *un escritor.*"

"What will I write? Comics?"

"Books. *Muchos libros.*"

"I think I might design toys."

Abuela shrugged. "*Cada juegete tiene un* story."

I only played with my toys in her house because I felt comfortable there. When my father was home, he'd shoot me weird looks when I would fly down the hall with my soaring silver-armored action figure ROM the Spaceknight, a cyborg warrior intent on protecting his people on the planet Galador from the invading and ultraviolent Dire Wraiths. In the Marvel-licensed comic that I picked up for 40 cents every month at the corner bodega, ROM pursues the enemy to Earth and is now responsible for hunting down the monstrous aliens before they succeed in conquering humanity. ROM's neutralizing blaster blinked and beeped, and I was careful not to overuse the weapon for fear that its batteries would wear down. It was loud enough that if I triggered it in the living room where my Anglo father played his vinyl records—Rollings Stones' *Tattoo You*, Phil Collins' *Face Value*—he'd tell me to go play outside. I didn't want the older kids in the neighborhood to judge me, to deem me a toy-obsessed child, so I went to abuela's house, where my imagination and my arrested behavior had no limits. Where I could play with any toy and draw any comic and watch any pop-culture TV show or movie—my favorite at that time being Japanese-animation shows like *Battle of the Planets* and *Star Blazers*.

Abuela married a tough, uncompromising Ybor City native—and a bit of a con man. My abuelo ran a tire shop where he regrooved old discarded tires with a grooving iron and resold them in an impov-

Essays & Poems

erished neighborhood a few miles from our own. In my twenties, I would learn from his family that he was mobbed up and that he operated a whorehouse in Tampa for many years. He was, in other words, a handful, but she kept him in line for as long as I knew them, and she didn't tolerate bad behavior from strangers.

Once, my mother was driving us to the mall for school clothes; my abuela sat in the passenger seat, me in the backseat. Mom wasn't driving fast enough to suit a cluster of four Outlaws bikers and their ladies riding, well, bitch. All four denim-clad cyclists sped around our 1974 AMC Matador to reach the red light before we did, and an unhelmeted, sunglassed woman turned around, giving my mother the middle finger.

This set off my abuela.

"Shitpots!" she screamed at the bikers, having cranked her window down to allow them to better hear her strange insult. "You're all shitpots!"

This made me nervous, but the bikers only shook their heads and laughed before frapping their engines and tearing off with the green light.

"*Maricones*," she muttered, rolling up her window.

I resumed reading my ROM comic book and playing with my ROM action figure. In order to change the mood, my mother turned up the car-dash volume on the Police's "Every Breath You Take." I looked for Wraiths to neutralize and sang along with Sting.

Abuela let out a big sigh, then said: "I think I'll make *croquetas* tonight."

Come back to me, *abuelita*.

As I grew older, I began spending more time with my friends in the beige suburbs, friends who had big garages for things like drum kits and PA systems. My mother bought me a bass guitar and an amplifier; she would drive me to the tract houses thirty minutes away from downtown. Eventually I started a rock band called Voodoo Fetus with a drummer and a guitarist. We covered Jimi Hendrix songs badly, did our best to mimic basic riff-rock like "Wild Thing" and "Sunshine of Your Love." We were awful; we only progressively got better through sheer will power and the inordinate time we spent repeatedly rehears-

The Book of Life After Death

ing those songs. Over dinner, Abuela would sometimes say that she missed watching TV with me, but I sensed that she understood how adolescence works. Perhaps too well.

"My sister's son was in a band years ago," she revealed to me once. "But his friends didn't play their instruments much. They'd sit around and look at porno tapes together."

I nearly blew *picadillo* through my nose. "Abuela!"

"*Perdone*," she said, smiling. "*Es la verdad!*"

"OK, *pero* come on! I have to eat!"

She laughed and poured me a Malta Hatuey, which grossed me out unless I drank one in her kitchen. Everything tasted better in *la cocina*. Everything still does.

How do I get back there?

Abuela died when I was in graduate school at Florida State University in Tallahassee, Florida, writing my dissertation. I thought about her nearly every day. I spent word processing my thoughts, my insights on storytelling and pop culture.

I thought she had more time, that *we* had more time, but I miscalculated. She died quietly in her bedroom one evening as I put the finishing touches on my manuscript, which had been accepted for publication by a small literary press in San Francisco.

I wept for an hour, then stopped. My tears resumed 30 years later as I put these words into a Word doc, a plastic cup of white-people Starbucks beside my MacBook. It tastes fake, but I need the caffeine, so I keep sipping.

I do a few push-ups.

I moonwalk across the tiled floor of the kitchen of my own house in downtown Las Vegas.

I flip through a ROM comic book.

I use the Internet to print out a recipe for *ropa vieja*; the instructions are magnetized to my fridge. I don't do so much as touch a frying pan.

I watch the *nunchaku* episode of *That's Incredible* on YouTube and cry again.

I look at my bookshelf and consider the number of books with my name on them.

I write another academic article for a journal devoted to the study

114

Essays & Poems

of pop culture.

I teach a class on comic books and spend an entire meeting discussing ROM.

She lives on in me, in everything I do and say, but she's not here with me.

I'll put them in the rack for you, abuelita.

TO MY GRANNY

Maeve Holler

You probably already know, but I finally went back to the Kiln. I sat in the gas station parking lot and thought of your spider veins, the sun in your blood. I went back to the blue — to the sinking swampland playground. I ate jumbo watermelons and boiled peanuts, watched kids play kick-the-can while hurricanes of red dirt eddied through the August air. I thought of your escape, your return. Your husband before grandpa. The babies you were forced to leave behind. The frantic midnight ride to Georgia. The throbbing pieces of you hidden throughout the earth, lying dormant & raw in the river silt like splintered glass. I imagined what it would be like if we could press a record of your memories and play them back: the running dead, an identity change, all the white lies, your lost birth certificate, the throwing knives. Like the broken chicken necks, they're all mythology & blurred lore for me. But, paralyzed in the thick of Mississippi, I wish to inherit the storm that brewed inside of you: the one that ricochets inside of me. They all say I look just like you — hard eyes, sharp teeth, knitted lips. And I know in my chest that we are two serpentine sisters, birthed from the same flow of angry ancestral foam. I am a mirror of you, slithering in the forest, lost and trying to find a root. Any root. So I dig, and I dig, and I look, but my hands keep coming up empty. Is this the barren soil of you? Of me?

Essays & Poems

THE TRAIN TRACKS REACHED

Stacey Balkun

as far as we could see, stretching
into what was left of the forest.
I startle awake with a pulse

in my palm as if you had grabbed
my hand, pulling me to the platform
clutching both our tickets.

The fate line diverges
from the lifeline.

I won't find a concert stub
in my pocket, dated
from that last night together.

Post oak, bur oak, scarlet oak.

There were so many blue and white
lights flashing on the band
we thought we had entered

the future. For a second
I thought you lived

across the street from me.
From my window, I swear
I saw you smoking

in your driveway, waiting
for a cab and I just watched
you, not crossing

The Book of Life After Death

the cracked pavement
even for a light.

Willow oak, water oak, laurel oak,

I've stopped denying
anything: I did swim
in the soiled creek.

The rabbits wore crowns
of woven clover.
Jim, I loved you

for so long I think
I still do, this ten-year hunger
to take back my Cure cassette

from your car, where as far
as I know, it's still half-
unspooled in the tape deck

stuck how it was when we found
your body hung limp
in the cold morning.

Silver oak, blackjack oak, everything

is a gamble,
our old search
for couch quarters,

taking too long
to lock our bikes
at the station, hearing

the shriek of the rails
just around the bend, the lean

Essays & Poems

in for a kiss on the cheek.

I regret not taking your hand.

*Live oak, canyon live oak, interior
live oak,* the trees are not
what I want alive.

The forest is half gone,
condos pale in the white sun.
The trains keep to their schedule.

There is no distance, only time.

The name of the album I'll never get back
was *Kiss me, Kiss me, Kiss me.*

Italicized lines from *The Trees of North America*, C. Frank Brockman, 1968

CONTRIBUTORS

Celia Lisset Alvarez has four collections of poetry, *Shapeshifting* (winner of the 2005 Spire Press Poetry Award), *The Stones* (Finishing Line Press 2006), *Multiverses* (Finishing Line Press 2021, a finalist in the narrative poetry category of American Book Fest's Best Books Award) and *Bodies & Words* (Assure Press 2022). Her stories and poetry have appeared in numerous journals and anthologies. She teaches at Our Lady of Lourdes Academy.

Pam Anderson spent 30 years helping young people with their writing as a high school English teacher, retired, and decided to dedicate energy to her own work. She has completed her MFA in Creative Nonfiction at Sierra Nevada University. Her essays, interviews, and criticisms have appeared in *Manifest-Station*, *HEAL*, *Bookends Review*, *Prospectus*, and *Chicago Review of Books*.

C. Prudence Arceneaux, a native Texan, is a poet who teaches English and Creative Writing at Austin Community College in Austin, TX. Her work has appeared in various journals, including *Limestone*, *New Texas*, *Hazmat Review*, *Texas Observer*, *Whiskey Island Magazine*, *African Voices* and *Inkwell*. She is the author of two chapbooks of poetry—*Dirt* (awarded the 2018 Jean Pedrick Prize) and *Liberty*.

Stacey Balkun is the author of *Sweetbitter* & co-editor of *Fiolet & Wing*. Winner of the 2019 New South Writing Contest, her work has appeared in *Mississippi Review*, *Pleiades*, & several other anthologies & journals. Stacey holds an MFA from Fresno State & teaches online at The Poetry Barn. She currently works as Coordinator for the Graduate and Undergraduate English programs at the University of New Orleans.

DeAnna Beachley teaches U.S. History and Women's Studies at the College of Southern Nevada. Primarily a poet, she has recently been working on creative nonfiction essays. Her poetry has appeared in *Red Rock Review*, *Parks and Points*, the *Kenyon Review Blog*, *Sandstone & Silver*, *Thimble*, *The Ekphrastic Review Challenge*, *300 Days of Sun*, *Slant*, and *Gyroscope Review*, and is forthcoming in two anthologies. Her work has won awards and has been included in an art/poetry exhibit, *A Room of Her Own*. When not teaching or writing, she enjoys hiking and bird watching.

Chloe Biggs received her MFA in Creative Writing from Fairleigh Dickinson University, where she also served as the Editorial Assistant in poetry for *The Literary Review*. Born and raised in the San Francisco Bay area, she recently moved back home after a stint in New York City. When she isn't at work (teaching high school English and Drama), she can be found attempting to finish writing one of the novels she has outlined, reading gothic lit, listening to emo and punk music, and celebrating Halloween 365 days per year.

James Joseph Brown holds an MFA from the University of Nevada, Las Vegas. His essays, poems, and short stories have appeared in *The Stockholm Review of Literature*, *Desert Companion*, *Santa Fe Literary Review*, *Red Rock Review*, and other publications. He has lived and worked in Russia, South Korea, Thailand, Kuwait, and Saudi Arabia, where he currently works as an English Instructor. Visit him at www.jamesjosephbrown.com.

Cathleen Calbert's writing has appeared in *Ms.*, *The Nation*, *The New York Times*, *The Paris Review*, *Poetry*, and elsewhere. She is the author of four books of poems: *Lessons in Space*, *Bad Judgment*, *Sleeping with a Famous Poet*, and *The Afflicted Girls*. Her awards include the 92nd Street Y Discovery Poetry Prize, a Pushcart Prize, the Sheila Motton Book Prize, and the Mary Tucker Thorp Professorship at Rhode Island College.

Linda Michel Cassidy is from Arroyo Seco, NM, a place downright saturated with ghosts. Her writing appears or is upcoming in *Rattle*, *Painted Bride*, *Eleven Eleven*, and others.

Susan Cohen's work has appeared in *Manifest-Station*, *Six Hens*, *Adanna Literary Review*, *All Things Girl*, and *Cyclamens and Swords*, and has been shortlisted twice for the *Glimmer Train* short story awards.

Andrew Collard's poems have appeared in *Ploughshares*, *Best New Poets*, *VQR*, and elsewhere. He lives in Grand Rapids, MI, and is a PhD candidate at Western Michigan University. He is currently the poetry editor for *Third Coast*.

Flower Conroy is an LGBTQIA+ writer, NEA and MacDowell Fellow, and former Key West Poet Laureate. Flower Conroy's first full-length manuscript, *Snake Breaking Medusa Disorder*, was chosen by Chen Chen as the winner of the Stevens Manuscript Competition; her second collection, *A Sentimental Hairpin*, was published by Tolsun Books. Her poetry will or has appeared in *American Poetry Review*, *New England Review*, *Prairie Schooner*, *Michigan Quarterly*

Review, and others. Her third book, *Greenest Grass*, was the winner of the Blue Lynx Prize.

Letisia Cruz is a Cuban-American writer and artist. She is the author of *The Lost Girls Book of Divination* (Tolsun Books, 2018). Her poetry manuscript, *Migrations & Other Exiles*, was awarded the 2022 Idaho Prize for Poetry and is forthcoming in 2023 from Lost Horse Press. She is the recipient of a 2022 artist grant from the St. Petersburg Arts Alliance and was selected as a 2022 Dali Dozen Emerging Artist Exhibition participant for her project *Rituales: An Exploration of Faith in the Caribbean*. She is a graduate of Fairleigh Dickinson University's MFA program and a member of the Artist Enclave of Historic Kenwood (AEHK). She lives in St. Petersburg, Florida with her partner and their cats, plants, and several hundred lizards. Find more of her work at lesinfin.com.

Deidra Suwanee Dees, Ed.D. and her family descend from Hotvlkvlke (Wind Clan) following Muscogee stompdance traditions. She serves as Director/Tribal Archivist at the Poarch Band of Creek Indians. She teaches Native American Studies at University of South Alabama, Tribally sponsored. She writes for the *Creek Corner Magazine*. Heleswv heres, mvto.

Lisa del Rosso originally trained as a classical singer and completed a post-graduate program at LAMDA (London Academy of Music and Dramatic Art), living and performing in London before moving to New York City. Her plays *Clare's Room* and *Samaritan* have been performed Off-Broadway and had public readings, while "St. John," her third play, was a semi-finalist for the 2011 Eugene O'Neill National Playwrights Conference. Her writing has appeared in *The New York Times*, *The Night Heron Barks*, *Ran Off With the Star Bassoon*, *Barking Sycamores Neurodivergent Literature*, *The Chillfiltr Review*, *Sowing Creek Press*, *The Literary Traveler*, *Serving House Journal*, *Vietnam-WarPoetry*, *Young Minds Magazine* (London/UK), *Time Out New York*, *The Huffington Post*, *The Neue Rundschau* (Germany), *Jetlag Café* (Germany), and *One Magazine* (London/UK), for whom she writes theater reviews. Her first book, *Confessions of an Accidental Professor*, was published in 2018, and she had the pleasure of being interviewed about the book by Brian Lehrer on his WNYC radio program. Her second essays-in-memoir book, *You Are All a Part of Me*, was published in early 2021. She is the recipient of a 2018 NYU College of Arts & Sciences Teaching Award, where she currently teaches writing. In 2019, she was awarded a New York Writers Workshop scholarship to Sardinia.

Flynn Dexter is published in *Clark: Poetry from Clark County, Nevada*, and *Sandstone and Silver: An Anthology of Nevada Poets*. Flynn has been a poetry educator for Nevada students, Individual Slam Champion, 7+ year experienced host/emcee, and community organizer of the Human Experience open mic. Their poetry centers around LGBTQ+ life, grief and loss, healing, love, and spirituality. Rooted in ordinary experiences, they work to shed light on the brilliance and significance of everyday life.

Rebecca Douglas is an Australian writer whose essays, articles, reviews, and fiction have been published by *Overland Journal, Kill Your Darlings, The Australian, The Sydney Morning Herald, The Guardian, ELLE, The Big Issue,* and many other lovely places.

Sarah Chavera Edwards is a Chicana writer based in Phoenix, Arizona. Her creative writing has been published in *TERSE Journal, The Nasiona, The Dewdrop,* and *The Roadrunner Review*. She also writes articles for national publications such as *Newsweek, Ms. Magazine, Healthline,* and more.

Farnaz Fatemi, an Iranian American poet, editor & writing teacher, is a founding member of The Hive Poetry Collective in Santa Cruz, CA. Her book, *Sister Tongue* زبان خواهر , was published in September 2022. It won the 2021 Stan and Tom Wick Poetry Prize, selected by Tracy K. Smith, and received a Starred Review from *Publisher's Weekly*. Some of her work appears in *Poem-a-Day (Poets.org), Tab Journal, Pedestal Review, Nowruz Journal,* and *Tupelo Quarterly* and the anthologies *Essential Voices: Poetry of Iran and its Diaspora* and *Halal If You Hear Me*. More at farnazfatemi.com

Kelly Jean Fitzsimmons is a writer, educator, and storyteller who lives in Astoria, Queens. Her nonfiction work has appeared in *HiLoBrow, Human Parts, Marie Claire,* and *Hippocampus Magazine*, among others. Her most recent play, a superhero comedy, *All I Want Is One More Meanwhile...* made its Midwest premiere at Otherworld Theatre in Chicago. After a decade of supporting AP teachers and coordinators behind the scenes with the Advanced Placement Program at the College Board, she stepped back into the classroom. Now she designs and teaches writing workshops for students of all ages. Her specialty is helping high school students craft meaningful college application essays that highlight their unique character for admissions officers. Earning an MFA in Creative Nonfiction from Fairleigh Dickinson University, Kelly Jean combined her love for theater and narrative nonfiction to create *No, YOU Tell It!* Subscribe to the podcast at noyoutellit.com, or your preferred platform, and share it with a friend!

Audrey Forbes is a poet born and raised in the city of sin where she repents through her pen. Her work stitches together themes on womanhood, grief, and love in an attempt to make something of her wonder. She received her B.A. from the University of Nevada, Las Vegas in English. Most recently, her poetry has been featured in *Apricity Press* and *pacificREVIEW*.

Robert René Galván, born in San Antonio, resides in New York City where he works as a professional musician and poet. His collections of poems are *Meteors* (Lux Nova Press) and *Undesirable: Race and Remembrance*, (Somos en Escrito Foundation Press), *Standing Stones*, (Finishing Line Press), and *The Shadow of Time* (Adelaide Books). His poetry has been featured in such publications as *The Acentos Review, Adelaide Literary Magazine, Azahares Literary Magazine, Gyroscope, Hawaii Review, Hispanic Culture Review, Latino Book Review, Newtown Review, Panoply, Prachya Review, Sequestrum, Shoreline of Infinity, Somos en Escrito, Stillwater Review, West Texas Literary Review*, and *UU World*. He is a Shortlist Winner Nominee in the 2018 Adelaide Literary Award for Best Poem. Recently, his poems are featured in *Puro ChicanX Writers of the 21st Century (2nd Edition)* and in *Yellow Medicine Review: A Journal of Indigenous Literature, Art and Thought*. His poems have been nominated for Best of Web and the Pushcart Prize. His poem, "Awakening," was featured in the author's voice on NPR as part of National Poetry Month in the Spring of 2021.

Nancy Gott graduated from The University of Iowa with an undergraduate degree in English, where she studied creative and poetry writing. Her work has been published in *Qarrtsiluni, Ekphrastic Review Challenge*, and numerous local publications in Las Vegas, as a freelance writer. Additionally, many of her zany prose pieces aired on the local NPR affiliate, KNPR's *Making Nevada Home* in the early 2000s. Recently, she was interviewed for a local TV show by Clark County Poet Laureate, Heather Lang-Cassera, with whom she collaborated on a community-wide pandemic poem, as well as a poetry project for a local park that will feature poems carved in concrete surfaces.

Courtney Harler is a freelance writer, editor, and educator based in Las Vegas, Nevada. She holds an MFA from Sierra Nevada University (2017) and an MA from Eastern Washington University (2013). Courtney has been honored by fellowships from Writing By Writers, Community of Writers, Napa Valley Writers' Conference, and Nevada Arts Council. Courtney's written work—which includes poems, flash fictions, short stories, literary analyses, craft essays, book and film reviews, author interviews, personal essays, and hybrid pieces—has been published around the world. Links to her publications and other related awards can be found at https://harlerliterary.llc.

Hunter Hazelton was born and raised in Phoenix, Arizona. He holds a BSED from Northern Arizona University. After studying abroad in Norwich, England, he composed his debut collection of work, *I Never Understood Religion Until I Learned Your Name* (Tolsun Books 2021). Other poems have been published by *Best New Poets*, *Scribendi*, among others. Currently, he teaches high school English. He was born in 1998.

Maeve Holler is an editor, writer, poet, and educator living in New Orleans, Louisiana. Her debut poetry collection, *HOW TO LEAVE YOUR FAMILY*, is forthcoming from Finishing Line Press, and her writing has appeared in *The Boiler Journal, Leveler, Scalawag Magazine, The Cardiff Review, Wildness,* and elsewhere. Maeve is the recipient of the 2020 Alfred Boas Poetry Prize and was most recently nominated for a 2022 Pushcart Prize. She holds an MFA in Creative Writing from the University of Miami and a BA in English and Gender & Sexuality Studies from Tulane University.

Alexis Ivy is a 2018 recipient of the Massachusetts Cultural Council Fellowship in Poetry and the author of *Romance with Small-Time Crooks* (BlazeVOX [books], 2013), and *Taking the Homeless Census* (Saturnalia Books, 2020) which won the 2018 Saturnalia Editors Prize. Her poems have recently appeared in *Saranac Review, Poet Lore* and *Sugar House Review*. She is an advocate for the homeless in her hometown, Boston.

Sarah Johnson received her PhD in Writing and Rhetoric from George Mason University and also holds an MFA in Creative Writing from American University. Her academic work has been featured in *Praxis: A Writing Center Journal, College Composition and Communication*, and others. Her creative work has appeared in *The Worcester Review, District Lit, High Shelf Press*, and others.

Leah Claire Kaminski is the author of three chapbooks, from Harbor Editions, Milk and Cake Press, and Dancing Girl Press. Poems appear in places like *Bennington Review, Boston Review, Harvard Review, Prairie Schooner,* and *The Rumpus*. Leah is poetry editor for The Dodge and lives in Chicago with her family.

Jen Karetnick's fourth full-length book is *The Burning Where Breath Used to*

Be (David Robert Books, September 2020), a CIPA EVVY winner, an Eric Hoffer Poetry Category Finalist, and a Kops Fetherling Honorable Mention. She is also the author of *Hunger Until It's Pain* (Salmon Poetry, Spring 2023) in addition to six other collections. Long-listed for the international 2021 Alpine Fellowship Writing Prize and recipient of a Merit Award in the Atlanta Review 2021 International Poetry Competition, she has won the Tiferet Writing Contest for Poetry, Split Rock Review Chapbook Competition, Hart Crane Memorial Prize, and Anna Davidson Rosenberg Prize, among others. Co-founder and managing editor of *SWWIM Every Day*, she has had work in *The Comstock Review*, *december*, *Michigan Quarterly Review*, *The Missouri Review Poem of the Week*, *Poet Lore*, *Terrain.org*, and elsewhere. Based in Miami, she works as a restaurant critic, lifestyle journalist, and author of four cookbooks, four guidebooks, and more. See jkaretnick.com.

Kelly Kaur's novel, *Letters to Singapore*, was published by Stonehouse Publishing, May 2022. Her poems and works have been published internationally: *Understorey Magazine*, on Blindman Session Beer Cans, *Best Asian Stories 2020*, *Let In the Light*, Asia Anthology, *Best Asian Poetry 2021-2022*, IHRAF Publishes (International Human Rights Arts Festival, New York 2021 and 2022), The North Dakota Human Rights Arts Festival Travelling Exhibition in 6 cities, January to November 2022, Growing Up Indian (Singapore Anthology 2022), and *Landed: Transformative Stories of Canadian Immigrant Women* (September 2022). Kelly's poem, "The Justice of Death," was awarded Honorable Mention in the Creators of Justice Literary Awards, International Human Rights Art Festival, New York. Her story, "The Kitchen is Her Home," was published in *Heart/h*, Home Anthology in United Kingdom, October 2021; it was nominated for the Pushcart Prize 2022. Her works are on the Lunar Codex project: her poem, "A Singaporean's Love Affair" is going to the moon on the NOVA Mission on the NOVA time capsule in 2023. *Letters to Singapore* will also be going to the moon on the Griffin Mission on the Polaris time capsule in 2023/2024.

Arthur Kayzakian was born in Tehran, Iran on a war-torn block. His first experiences of earth are machine gun fire and sirens. They turned off the lights and closed the blinds to avoid uniformed guards and weaponry that targeted visible homes. Due to the urgent nature of our situation in Iran, his parents did the best they could to raise him, and as a result, he lives with a deep sense of unrest, of disband, and the absence of a homeland. His family sought political asylum in London when he turned three years old to escape the Iranian Revolution. He started writing verse in sixth grade as a form of song, but what he knows now is his use of language has always been a way for him to make sense of war and trauma. He has protected himself with poetry, and he writes poems from a shattered lyric to reflect his chaotic upbringing. He did not know any other way to remedy the memories in his body. Poetry for him is a form of survival, and he aims to continue his work as a poet in his fight against history, against the state, and the use of normative language. His working manuscript is a book of poems that integrate his personal history with the one the state gave him. He has been writing poems about the Irani-an-Armenian experience, which is erased from Iranian and Armenian people, since it falls in between both identities as a race and culture.

Jarret Keene is an Assistant Professor in the English Department at the University of Nevada, Las Vegas, where he teaches American literature and the graphic novel. He has written books—travel guide, rock-band biography, poetry collections—and edited short-fiction anthologies such as *Las Vegas Noir* and *Dead Neon: Tales of Near-Future Las Vegas*.

Susan L. Leary is the author of three poetry collections: *A Buffet Table Fit for Queens*, winner of The Washburn Prize and forthcoming from Harbor Review / Small Harbor Publishing; *Contraband Paradise* (Main Street Rag, 2021); and *This Girl, Your Disciple* (Finishing Line Press, 2019), finalist for The Heartland Review Press Chapbook Prize and semi-finalist for the Elyse Wolf Prize with Slate Roof Press. Her work has appeared in such places as *Tar River Poetry, Superstition Review, Tahoma Literary Review*, and *Pithead Chapel*. Recently, she was a finalist for the 16th Mudfish Poetry Prize, judged by Marie Howe. She teaches Writing Studies at the University of Miami.

Xiaoly Li is a poet and photographer who lives in Massachusetts. She is a 2022 recipient of the Massachusetts Cultural Council Artist Fellowship Grant in Poetry. Prior to writing poetry, she published stories in a selection of Chinese newspapers. Her photography, which has been shown and sold in galleries in Boston, often accompanies her poems. Her poetry has recently appeared in *Spillway, American Journal of Poetry, PANK, Atlanta Review, Chautauqua, Rhino, Cold Mountain Review, J Journal* and elsewhere. Her work has been featured on Verse Daily and in several anthologies. She has been nominated for Best of the Net three times, Best New Poets, and a Pushcart Prize. Xiaoly received her Ph.D. in electrical engineering from Worcester Polytechnic Institute and her master's in computer science and engineering from Tsinghua University in China.

Shane Mason has always dabbled in writing but never formalized nor submitted any works. While battling cholangiocarcinoma, he was inspired to write "Questions on Death" and encouraged to submit it by his cousin (often referred to as sister), renowned poet Flower Conroy. He currently resides in Harrison, NJ with his husband, writer James R Lynch, and is in remission since being blessed with an organ transplant.

Charlene Stegman Moskal is a Teaching Artist with The Alzheimer's Poetry Project under the auspices of the Poetry Promise Organization, Las Vegas. She's published in numerous anthologies, print magazines, and online, including *Dark of Winter* (Milk & Cake Press), *Sandstone & Silver: An Anthology of Nevada Poets* (Zeitgeist Press), and *Humana Obscura* (issues 1 & 2). Her first chapbook is *One Bare Foot* (Zeitgeist Press), with a second, *Leavings from My Table*, from Finishing Line Press in 2022. She's in her seventh decade, laughs a lot, and really likes coffee hot fudge sundaes.

Colin Pope's most recent collection of poetry is *Prayer Book for the New Heretic* (NYQ Books, 2023). Poems, essays, and criticism have appeared in journals and publications such as *The Kenyon Review, Slate, The Gettysburg Review, West Branch, AGNI, Ninth Letter, Third Coast, Pleiades, Willow Springs, Best New Poets,* and others. Colin is Assistant Director of Creative Writing at Northwestern University and serves on the editorial board of *Nimrod International.*

Bryan Price is the author of the forthcoming collection of elegies, *A Plea for Secular Gods* (What Books Press, 2023). His work has appeared in *UCity Review, Posit,* and *Rhino Poetry* (among others). He lives and teaches in Southern California.

Dani Putney is a queer, non-binary, mixed-race Filipinx, & neurodivergent poet originally from Sacramento, California. Their debut poetry collection, *Salamat sa Intersectionality* (Okay Donkey Press, 2021), is a finalist for the 2022 Lambda Literary Award in Transgender Poetry. They've also published a poetry chapbook, *Dela Torre* (Sundress Publications, 2022). While not always there, they reside in the Nevada desert.

Elizabeth Quiñones-Zaldaña is a southern Nevada writer and educator. She leads poetry and art workshops in her local community. Her poems have been published in *Sagebrush to Sandstone: A Humanities Guide to Outdoor Nevada,* Nevada Public Radio's *Desert Companion, 300 Days of Sun,* and elsewhere. Her poetry collection, *Bougainvillea,* is available through Tolsun Books.

Andrew Revie is a poet living in Rockland County, NY. He graduated from William Paterson University with a BA in writing and later earned an MFA in poetry from Fairleigh Dickinson University. His work has previously appeared in *Petite Hound Press* and *The Night Heron Barks*. In 2016 he was nominated for a Pushcart Prize.

Arnisha Royston's goal as a Black poet and writer is to extend the understanding of poetry and its relationship to the African American community, while using her experiences as a writer to explore how form, expression, emotion, and vulnerability are interwoven into Black narratives. She is a second year MFA student at San Diego State University, where she is a Master's Research fellow, a Graduate English Fellow, and a Teaching Associate. Moreover, three of her poems, "Claiming the Parts," "Souvenirs for the Dead," and "Who Breaks Up in a Diner" are forthcoming in Zone 3 Press.

Paul Skenazy taught literature and writing at the University of California, Santa Cruz. He is the author of *Temper, CA*, the winner of the Miami University Press Novella Contest, 2018, and *Still Life* (Paper Angel Press, 2021).

Dulce Solis is a Mexican writer, and former journalist. She has published the following short stories in anthologies: "La Mosquita Justiciera," "Feminicidio," and "La Bruja Mestiza." She is also the author of the book *Manual de Autodefensa Femenina* available on Amazon. Additionally she produces the literature Podcast *Mujeres Mágicas*. Dulce was born and raised in Michoacán, Mexico. She attended school for journalism and later obtained her master's degree in creative marketing. Dulce has always been passionate about writing and she loves to share her stories with others. Dulce currently resides in Las Vegas with her husband and young son. In her spare time, she enjoys reading, writing, and meditating. Dulce loves the colors blue and green, and she feels lucky to be surrounded by so much magic in her life.

Ellen Sollinger Walker is a retired classical pianist and psychologist living in Clearwater, Florida. She writes short fiction, creative non-fiction, poetry, and has recently finished her first novella. Her short stories may be found in *Dillydoun Review, Change Seven Literary Magazine, The Pigeon Review Literary and Art Magazine, Vine Leaves Press*, and *Storytellers Refrain*. She won Honorable Mention in the 2021 Dillydoun International Fiction Contest.

Will Stenberg is a poet, screenwriter, and musician who grew up in a small logging town in the wilds of Northern California and currently resides in

Portland, Oregon. His work has been featured in *Otis Nebula, Sybil Journal, Parhelion Literary Magazine,* and elsewhere, and his poetry collection *No Comebacks* was published in 2019 by Yellow Lark Press in Austin, Texas.

Jesse Arthur Stone's poems have appeared in ILDS 2019 White Mice Poetry Contest, *Inlandia: A Literary Journey, Rabbit* (Australia), *Edge, Nimrod; Passager, Ilya's Honey, Peralta Press, Treasure House, Vermont Voices, North By Northeast, The Observer* (London), *CrossCountry* (Montreal), *Artemis,* and *Hayden's Ferry Review.* He has won awards from: Arvon International Poetry Competition, *Artemis, Atlanta Review, Dallas Poets Community,* International Lawrence Durrell Society, Paumanok Poetry Award, West Virginia Writers, and was a semi-finalist in the 2019 and 2021 Hillary Gravendyk Prize Poetry Book Competitions. Stone was born in Long Beach, California and grew up in the Mojave Desert. He lives in West Virginia with his wife, Lynn Swanson, a poet, short story writer, novelist, and dance instructor.

Ashley Vargas, also known by her stage name, **Ms.AyeVee**, is an award-winning Afro-latina Literary Artist from Las Vegas, NV. She is a woman of many hats with a passion for Poetry. Her work has been featured by the legendary *All Def Poetry, Write About Now,* and *Button Poetry.* She has been published by Bookleaf Publishing, *The Red Rock Review,* Zeitgeist-Press, Hardy Publications, and Nevada State College. In 2020, Ms.AyeVee was recognized by Nevada Public Radio's *Desert Companion* magazine for their annual "Ones to Watch" issue. Also in 2020, she founded an online poetry competition called Beyond The Neon Poetry Slam that has since grown into a poetry anthology series and poetry festival. In 2021 she was nominated for The Crystal Bookmark Award from the Las Vegas Book Festival for advancing the cause of literacy and extraordinary literary achievement. That same year, she received Special Congressional Recognition from Nevada Rep. Susie Lee for Outstanding Poetry. In 2022 Ms.AyeVee released her new collection of poetry entitled *Broken Silence.* Please follow her poetic journey at https://linktr.ee/Msayevee.

Steve Wilson has several recent poems out or forthcoming in such journals as *Beloit Poetry Journal, Borderlands, Bluestem, Rio Grande Review, Cimarron Review, Commonweal, Poem, Georgetown Review, North American Review, America, The Christian Science Monitor, Blue Unicorn, New Orleans Review, San Pedro River Review, The Christian Century, New American Writing, Isotope: A Journal of Literary Nature and Science Writing, Midwest Quarterly, The Rio Grande Review,* and *New Letters;* as well as in a number of anthologies, including *O Taste and See: Food*

Poems (Bottom Dog Press), *Visiting Frost: Poems Inspired by Robert Frost* (University of Iowa), *Stories from Where We Live: The Gulf Coast* (Milkweed Editions), *Like Thunder: Poets Respond to Violence in America* (University of Iowa), *What Have You Lost?* (Greenwillow), *American Diaspora: Poetry of Displacement* (University of Iowa), *An Introduction to the Prose Poem* (Firewheel Editions), *Beloved on the Earth: 150 Poems of Grief and Gratitude* (Holy Cow! Press), *Classifieds: An Anthology of Prose Poems* (Equinox), *Improbable Worlds: An Anthology of Texas and Louisiana Poets* (Mutabilis), and *Going Down Grand: Poetry of the Grand Canyon* (Lithic). His books include *Allegory Dance*, *The Singapore Express*, *The Lost Seventh*, *Lose to Find*, and *The Reaches*, published in December 2019. His newest book, *Complicity*, was published in 2023.

Emilee Wirshing is a librarian and lifelong Nevadan. She advocates for local poets and creativity in the community by hosting various Poetry Open Mic Nights and writing workshops throughout Southern Nevada. She has served as a judge for the Library of Congress 'Letters About Literature' Contest and was the founding poetry editor of *Noble / Gas Qtrly*. Her poetry has been published in *300 Days of Sun*, *Infinite Rust*, *Quiddity*, *Helen*, and *Thing*. Anthologies *Clark*, *Legs of Tumbleweed*, *Wings of Lace*, and *Sandstone & Silver* also include her work. Tolsun Books released her chapbook, *american dream houses*, in March of 2020.

ACKNOWLEDGEMENTS

The following works have been previously published elsewhere:

"All Sales Are Final" by Andrew Revie was previously published by *The Night Heron Barks*.

"Elegy for a Gambler" by Jen Karetnick was previously published as a finalist for the 44th New Millennium Awards in *New Millennium Writings*.

"A Craft Talk" by Colin Pope was previously published in Volume 11 of the *Delmarva Review*.

"Welcoming the Light" by Jesse Arthur Stone was previously published in the Volume 41, Number 2, Spring/Summer 1998 issue of *Nimrod Journal of Prose & Poetry: A Range of Light, The Americas*.

"Mujeres Divinas/Divine Women" by Sarah Edwards was previously published in *The Roadrunner Review* where it received the 2021 Creative Nonfiction Prize.

"Roses in His Cheeks" by Lisa del Rosso was previously published in *You Are All a Part of Me* (Serving House Books, 2021).

"Mariner" by Emilee Wirshing was previously published in *300 Days of Sun*.

"To My Granny" by Maeve Holler also appears in *How to Leave Your Family* (Finishing Line Press, 2024).

CPSIA information can be obtained
at www.ICGtesting.com
Printed in the USA
BVHW091055010323
659313BV00003B/25